Verse by Verse Commentary on

1-2 TIMOTHY,

TITUS,

AND

PHILEMON

Enduring Word Commentary Series
By David Guzik

*The grass withers, the flower fades,
but the word of our God stands forever.*
Isaiah 40:8

Commentary on 1-2 Timothy, Titus, and Philemon

Copyright ©2019 by David Guzik

Printed in the United States of America
or in the United Kingdom

Print Edition ISBN: 978-1-939466-21-1

Enduring Word

5662 Calle Real #184

Goleta, CA 93117

Electronic Mail: ewm@enduringword.com

Internet Home Page: www.enduringword.com

Scripture references, unless noted, are from the New King James Version of the Bible, copyright ©1979, 1980, 1982, Thomas Nelson, Inc., Publisher.

Contents

1 Timothy 1 - Fighting for the Faith

A. Introduction.

1. (1) The identity of the author, Paul.

Paul, an apostle of Jesus Christ, by the commandment of God our Savior and the Lord Jesus Christ, our hope.

a. **Paul, an apostle of Jesus Christ**: Paul, in his self-description, emphasized his credentials (**apostle**) and his authority (**by the commandment of God**). He did this both as a *personal encouragement* to Timothy and so the letter could be used as a letter of reference before the Ephesian Christians.

i. It seems that 1 Timothy was written by the Apostle Paul to Timothy sometime after his release from Roman imprisonment as described at the end of the Book of Acts, and was written from Macedonia (1 Timothy 1:3).

ii. Apparently, after his release (hoped for in Philemon 22 and Philippians 1:25-26 and 2:24), Paul returned to the city of Ephesus. There he discovered that during his absence Ephesus had become a storm center of false teaching. This was a sad fulfillment of the prediction he made to the Ephesian elders in Acts 20:29-30.

iii. Paul probably dealt with the false teachers personally, but soon found it necessary to leave for Macedonia. He then left Timothy in charge of affairs at Ephesus, as his own personal representative. He knew that Timothy had a difficult job to carry out, so he hoped that this letter would both equip and encourage him in the task.

iv. "The use of this official title is an indication that the Pastoral Epistles were not merely private letters, but were intended to be read to the Churches committed to the charge of Timothy." (White)

b. **Our Savior**: At that very time, the title **Savior** was used to honor the Roman Emperor. People called, and were forced to call, Caesar Nero

7

"savior." Paul made the identity of the *real* **Savior** clear: **God**, in the person of **the Lord Jesus Christ**.

> i. White on **by the commandment of God**: "Here it is to be noted that the *command* proceeds equally from God and Christ Jesus. This language could hardly have been used if St. Paul conceived of Christ Jesus as a creature."

2. (2) The identity of the recipient, Timothy.

To Timothy, a true son in the faith: Grace, mercy, *and* peace from God our Father and Jesus Christ our Lord.

> a. **To Timothy**: The Book of Acts tells us that Timothy came from Lystra, a city in the province of Galatia (16:1-3). He was the son of a Greek father (16:2) and a Jewish mother named Eunice (2 Timothy 2:5). His mother and grandmother taught him the Scriptures from the time of Timothy's youth (2 Timothy 1:5; 3:15).

> b. **A true son in the faith**: Paul could consider Timothy **a true son in the faith** because he probably led him and his mother to faith in Jesus on Paul's first missionary journey (Acts 14:8-20 and 16:1). This also expressed Paul's confidence in Timothy's integrity and faithfulness to the truth.

> c. **Grace, mercy, and peace**: This is a familiar greeting Paul used in his letters to congregations. Here, he also applied it to an individual. God grants His **grace, mercy, and peace** not only to churches, but also to the *individuals* who make up the churches.

> > i. Yet there is a difference. When Paul wrote to churches, he commonly only greeted them with **grace** and **peace**. To both Timothy (also in 2 Timothy 1:2) and Titus (Titus 1:4) he added **mercy** to the greeting.

> > ii. "Not only grace and peace, as to others. When we pray for ministers, we must be more than ordinarily earnest for them with God. These three are joined together only in the Epistles of Timothy and Titus." (Trapp)

B. Paul urges Timothy to remain in Ephesus.

1. (3-4) Stay in Ephesus and stay with the Scriptures.

As I urged you when I went into Macedonia—remain in Ephesus that you may charge some that they teach no other doctrine, nor give heed to fables and endless genealogies, which cause disputes rather than godly edification which is in faith.

> a. **Remain in Ephesus**: Though Timothy had a difficult task Paul wanted him to **remain in Ephesus** and continue the work. Before Paul left for

Macedonia, he **urged** Timothy to **remain,** even though the work was difficult.

i. Paul told Timothy to **remain in Ephesus** because it seemed that Timothy wanted to give up and run away. Most everyone in ministry deals with this at some time; for a few it is a constant affliction. There was probably both external pressure and internal pressure for him to leave.

ii. We can think of many reasons why Timothy might *not* want to **remain in Ephesus:**

- He might have missed Paul and wanted to be with his mentor.

- He might have been intimidated by following Paul's ministry.

- He seems to have been somewhat timid or reserved by nature and was perhaps intimidated by the challenge.

- He might have been discouraged by the normal difficulties of ministry.

- He might have questioned his own calling.

- He might have been frustrated by the distracting and competing doctrines swirling around the Christians in Ephesus.

iii. Despite all these reasons, there is no doubt that God – and the Apostle Paul – wanted Timothy to **remain in Ephesus,** and in the rest of 1 Timothy 1, Paul gave Timothy at least six reasons why he should stay there and finish the ministry God gave him to do.

- Because they need the truth (1 Timothy 1:3-7).

- Because you minister in a hard place (1 Timothy 1:8-11).

- Because God uses unworthy people (1 Timothy 1:12-16).

- Because you serve a great God (1 Timothy 1:17).

- Because you are in a battle and cannot surrender (1 Timothy 1:18).

- Because not everyone else does (1 Timothy 1:19-20).

iv. God will allow us to be in difficult situations. We must set our minds to meet the challenge, or we will surely give up. Many years ago a famous Arctic explorer put this ad in a London newspaper: "Men wanted for hazardous journey, small wages, bitter cold, long months of complete darkness, constant danger, safe return doubtful. Honor and recognition in case of success." Thousands of men responded to the appeal because they were willing to embrace a difficult job when called to do so by a great leader.

b. **That you may charge some that they teach no other doctrine**: Paul left Timothy with an important job to do, making it all the more important that he **remain in Ephesus**. The job was to make sure that correct **doctrine** was taught in Ephesus.

i. **No other doctrine**: Paul left the Ephesian Christians with a particular set of teachings (which he had received from Jesus and the Old Testament). He was concerned that Timothy did everything he could to make sure the Ephesians *continue* in that doctrine. This was the first reason why it was important that Timothy remain in Ephesus.

ii. Paul did this because **doctrine** is important to God and *should* be important to His people. Today, *what* one believes – that is, their **doctrine** - is remarkably *unimportant* to most people. This spirit of the modern age has also heavily influenced modern Christians. We live in a day where Pilate's question *What is truth?* (John 18:38) is answered, "Whatever it means to *you*." Yet truth is important to God and should be to His people.

c. **That you may charge some**: Paul's concern was not primarily that Timothy himself would begin to teach wrong doctrine. His concern was that Timothy would allow others to spread these other doctrines. Timothy had to stand firm against difficult people and **charge some that they teach no other doctrine**. No wonder Timothy felt like leaving Ephesus.

i. In the ancient Greek, **charge** is a military word. It means "To give strict orders from a commanding officer" (Wiersbe). Timothy wasn't to present the *option* of correct doctrine to these **some** in Ephesus. He was to *command* it like a military officer.

d. **Nor give heed to fables and endless genealogies**: It seems that the great danger of these teachings (**fables and endless genealogies**) was that they were *silly distractions*. Timothy had to **remain in Ephesus** so that he could command others to ignore these speculative and silly distractions.

i. It wasn't that there was an elaborate anti-Jesus theology rising in Ephesus. It was more that they tended to get carried away by emphasizing the wrong things. Paul wanted to prevent the corruption that came when people gave authority to **fables and endless genealogies** instead of true doctrine. *Silly distractions* were also dangerous, because they took the place of **godly edification which is in faith**.

ii. Perhaps the **endless genealogies** had to do with Gnostic-type theories of "emanations" from God. Perhaps they were connected with Jewish-type legalism that sought righteousness by virtue of one's ancestry. Or perhaps he had in mind doctrinal systems based on mystic readings of Old Testament genealogies.

iii. Ancient Jewish writings have been discovered which dig into the most complex genealogies, connecting them with wild speculations about spiritual mysteries. A consuming interest in these kinds of things will crowd out **godly edification which is in faith**.

e. **Cause disputes rather than godly edification**: The eventual fruit of these man-made diversions is evident. Though they may be popular and fascinating in the short term, in the long run they don't strengthen God's people in faith.

i. "Discourses that turn to no profit; a great many words and little sense; and that sense not worth the pains of hearing." (Clarke)

2. (5-7) The purpose of the commandment.

Now the purpose of the commandment is love from a pure heart, *from* a good conscience, and *from* sincere faith, from which some, having strayed, have turned aside to idle talk, desiring to be teachers of the law, understanding neither what they say nor the things which they affirm.

a. **The purpose of the commandment**: The purpose of the law is found in its inward work upon the heart, not in mere outward observance. Without this understanding, it is easy to become shallow legalists who are only concerned with outward performance and appearance.

b. **Love from a pure heart**: This suggests the idea that the problem in Ephesus was along Jewish-type legalistic lines. They misunderstood the commandment and the law.

i. If spending time in God's word does not produce **love from a pure heart**, a **good conscience**, or **sincere faith** in us, something is wrong. Legalism may make us twist God's word, so that instead of showing **love** we are harsh and judgmental; instead of having a **good conscience** we always feel condemned knowing we don't measure up; and instead of **sincere faith** we practically trust in our own ability to please God.

c. **Idle talk**: This probably has in mind vain speculations about the Scriptures, which may have had analytical and entertainment value but were never meant to be our spiritual diet.

i. In the King James Version, **idle talk** is translated *vain jangling* - the idea is of meaningless babble.

d. **Understanding neither what they say nor the things which they affirm**: The problem people in Ephesus did not even understand the implications of their own teaching.

3. (8-11) Paul's condemnation of legalists is not a condemnation of the law itself.

But we know that the law *is* good if one uses it lawfully, knowing this: that the law is not made for a righteous person, but for *the* lawless and insubordinate, for *the* ungodly and for sinners, for *the* unholy and profane, for murderers of fathers and murderers of mothers, for manslayers, for fornicators, for sodomites, for kidnappers, for liars, for perjurers, and if there is any other thing that is contrary to sound doctrine, according to the glorious gospel of the blessed God which was committed to my trust.

a. **But we know that the law is good if one uses it lawfully**: The purpose of the law is to show us our sin, not to lead us to righteousness (as in Galatians 3:24-25). It wasn't made for the **righteous person** (who walks by faith according to Galatians 3:11) but for the **lawless and insubordinate**, to show them their sin.

i. The idea isn't that the law has *nothing* to say to the **righteous person**, but that it especially speaks to the ungodly. On the phrase, **The law is not made for a righteous person**, Clarke observed that the word for **made** "Refers to the custom of writing laws on boards, and hanging them up in public places within reach of every man, that they might be read by all; thus all would see against whom the law *lay*."

b. **For the lawless and insubordinate, for the ungodly and for sinners**: In Paul's mind **sound doctrine** and right conduct are vitally connected. The sinful *actions* described in verses 9 and 10 are **contrary to sound doctrine**.

i. Many people will condemn anyone with standards — especially higher standards — as being a legalist. Having standards and keeping them does not make us legalists and obedience doesn't make us legalists. We are legalists when we think what we do is what makes us right before God.

c. **If there is any other thing that is contrary to sound doctrine**: The implication is that in Ephesus, the church existed in a culture marked by these sins listed in verses 9 and 10 and those teaching false doctrine in some way allowed or promoted this sinful lifestyle.

i. **If there is any other thing**: "For the apostle took no delight to mention more of this cursed crew; but leaves them to the law to handle and hamper them, as unruly beasts, dogs, lions, leopards, are chained and caged up that they may not do mischief" (Clarke).

ii. The apparently sinful environment of Ephesus shows us another reason why it was important for Timothy to *remain in Ephesus*. He should remain there *because* it was a difficult place to serve God and further the kingdom. He had to break up the fallow ground there, instead of running to an easier place to plow.

d. **According to the glorious gospel of the blessed God**: Though the law cannot bring righteousness, **the glorious gospel of the blessed God** can — a gospel that, in the words of Paul, was **committed to** his **trust**. He sensed his responsibility to preserve and guard the gospel, and to pass it on to Timothy and others.

C. Paul's personal experience of the gospel.

1. (12-14) Why was Paul entrusted with the gospel?

And I thank Christ Jesus our Lord who has enabled me, because He counted me faithful, putting *me* into the ministry, although I was formerly a blasphemer, a persecutor, and an insolent man; but I obtained mercy because I did *it* ignorantly in unbelief. And the grace of our Lord was exceedingly abundant, with faith and love which are in Christ Jesus.

a. **I thank Christ Jesus our Lord who has enabled me**: Paul was entrusted with the gospel because Jesus **enabled** Paul, and Paul thanked Jesus for that enabling. Paul was enabled for this ministry because he was **counted... faithful** for the ministry. Faithfulness made Paul ready to be used by God.

i. We often see our Christian service as a matter of volunteering. Yet as Christians, in regard to Jesus and His church, we are not volunteers. We are slaves. We are duty bound servants of Jesus, and faithfulness is expected of such servants.

ii. **He counted me faithful**: You don't have to be smart to be faithful; you don't have to be talented or gifted. Faithfulness is something very down-to-earth, and each of us can be faithful in the place God has placed us.

iii. Many people wait to be faithful. We tell ourselves, "I'll be faithful when I'm in such and such a position." That is foolish. We should be faithful right where we are at — our faithfulness is shown in the small things.

b. **Putting me into the ministry**: **Ministry** simply means "service." In the original language of the New Testament, there is nothing high or spiritual about the word. It just means to work hard and serve. Yet for this former blasphemer and persecutor of God's people, this was a great honor.

i. "After Paul was saved, he became a foremost saint. The Lord did not allot him a second-class place in the church. He had been the leading sinner, but his Lord did not, therefore, say, 'I save you, but I shall always remember your wickedness to your disadvantage.' Not so: he counted him faithful, putting him into the ministry and into the apostleship, so that he was not a whit behind the very chief of the apostles. Brother, there is no reason why, if you have gone very far in sin, you should not go equally far in usefulness." (Spurgeon)

c. **Although I was formerly**: Paul's past did not disqualify him from serving God. God's mercy and grace were enough to cover his past and enable him to serve God. We should never feel that our past makes us unable to be used by God.

i. With these words, Paul gave Timothy another reason to remain in Ephesus. It is likely that one reason Timothy wanted to leave Ephesus and his ministry there because he felt *unworthy* or *incapable* of the work. These words from Paul assured Timothy, "If there is anyone unworthy of disqualified, it should be me. Yet God found a way to use me, and He will use you also as you remain in Ephesus."

d. **Because I did it ignorantly in unbelief**: **Ignorance** and **unbelief** never *excuse* our sin, but they do invite God's **mercy**, because sin in **ignorance** and **unbelief** makes one *less* guilty than the believer who sins knowingly.

e. **The grace of our Lord was exceedingly abundant**: It was not Paul's **ignorance** that saved him; it was the **exceeding abundant** grace of God (God's *unmerited* favor).

2. (15) Paul summarizes his personal experience of the gospel.

This *is* a faithful saying and worthy of all acceptance, that Christ Jesus came into the world to save sinners, of whom I am chief.

a. **This is a faithful saying and worthy of all acceptance**: This unusual phrase introduces a statement of special importance. Paul used this phrase 5 times – all in the Pastoral Epistles.

b. **Christ Jesus came into the world to save sinners**: Jesus came to save **sinners**, not those living under the illusion of their own righteousness. As Jesus taught, it is the sick who need a physician (Mark 2:17).

i. Since Jesus came into the world to save **sinners**, this is the first necessary qualification for being a child of God - being a sinner.

Sinners are not disqualified from coming to God, because Jesus came to save *them*.

ii. We also see the great danger in taking the terms *sin* and *sinner* out of our vocabulary. Many preachers deliberately do this today, because they don't want to offend anyone from the pulpit. But if Jesus came to save sinners, shouldn't we identify who those sinners are? How else will they come to salvation?

iii. "Even those who recognize that Christ's work is to save admit that it is more difficult to believe that this salvation belongs to sinners. Our mind is always prone to dwell on our own worthiness and, as soon as our unworthiness becomes apparent, our confidence fails. Thus the more a man feels the burden of his sins, he ought with greater courage to betake himself to Christ, relying on what is here taught, that He came to bring salvation not to the righteous but to sinners." (Calvin)

b. **Of whom I am chief**: Paul's claim to be the **chief** of sinners was not an expression of a strange false humility. He genuinely felt his sins made him more accountable before God than others.

i. Aren't we all equally sinners? No; "All men are truly sinners, but all men are not equally sinners. They are all in the mire; but they have not all sunk to an equal depth in it" (Spurgeon).

ii. Paul felt – rightly so – that his sins were worse because he was responsible for the death, imprisonment, and suffering of Christians, whom he persecuted before his life was changed by Jesus (Acts 8:3; 9:1-2, 1 Corinthians 15:9, Galatians 1:13, Philippians 3:6).

iii. In Acts 26:11, Paul explained to Agrippa what might have been his worst sin: *And I punished them often in every synagogue and compelled them to blaspheme; and being exceedingly enraged against them, I persecuted them even to foreign cities.* He compelled others to blaspheme Jesus. "This, indeed, was a very horrible part of Saul's sinfulness. To destroy their bodies was bad enough, but to destroy their souls too- to compel them to blaspheme, to speak evil of that name which they confessed to be their joy and their hope, surely that was the worst form that even persecution could assume. He forced them under torture to abjure the Christ whom their hearts loved. As it were he was not content to kill them, but he must damn them too" (Spurgeon).

iv. There *are* worse kinds of sin; sins that harm God's people are especially bad in God's eyes. We must soberly consider if we are guilty, now or in the past, of harming God's people. "[God] remembers jests and scoffs leveled at his little ones, and he bids those who indulge in them to take heed. You had better offend a king than one of the Lord's little ones" (Spurgeon).

v. "Despair's head is cut off and stuck on a pole by the salvation of 'the chief of sinners.' No man can now say that he is too great a sinner to be saved, because the chief of sinners was saved eighteen hundred years ago. If the ringleader, the chief of the gang, has been washed in the precious blood, and is now in heaven, why not I? Why not *you?*" (Spurgeon)

3. (16) Paul saved as a pattern of mercy to others.

However, for this reason I obtained mercy, that in me first Jesus Christ might show all longsuffering, as a pattern to those who are going to believe on Him for everlasting life.

a. **However, for this reason I obtained mercy**: A man as bad as Paul was **obtained mercy**. This means that the door is open to others who are not as bad sinners as Paul was.

i. White expresses the idea of Paul: "Christ's longsuffering will never undergo a more severe test than it did in my case, so that no sinner need ever despair. Let us glorify God therefore."

b. **As a pattern to those who are going to believe on Him**: This explains another reason why God loves to save sinners. They become a **pattern** to those who are **going to believe on Him**. God wants others to see what He can do by working in us.

i. *This* truth – the doctrine - that changed Paul's life was the truth he commanded Timothy to guard earlier in the chapter.

ii. **As a pattern**: Paul, under the inspiration of the Holy Spirit, understood that his life, conversion, and service to God was in some way a **pattern** to other believers.

4. (17) Paul's praise to the God who saved him.

Now to the King eternal, immortal, invisible, to God who alone is wise, *be* honor and glory forever and ever. Amen.

a. **Now to the King eternal**: Paul could not think of how bad he was, and how great the salvation of God was, and how great the love of God was, without simply breaking into spontaneous praise.

b. **The King eternal, immortal, invisible, to God who alone is wise**: This outburst of praise shows that Paul both *knew* God and that he *loved* God.

i. He knew God to be **the King eternal**, ruling and reigning in complete power and glory.

ii. He knew God to be **immortal**, existing before anything else existed, and being the Creator of all things.

iii. He knew God to be **invisible**, not completely knowable by us; we can't completely figure out God, or know all His secrets.

iv. He knew God **alone is wise**, that He is God - and we are not. We think our plans and insights are so important, but only God really knows and understands all things.

c. **Be honor and glory forever and ever**: Knowing all this about God, Paul couldn't stop praising Him. If we ever have trouble worshipping God, it is because we don't know Him very well.

i. This description of God gave Timothy still another reason to remain in Ephesus. He could and should stay there when he considered the greatness of the God who he served. *This* great God was worthy of Timothy's sacrifice and could empower his service in Ephesus.

D. Paul's charge to Timothy: carry on the fight.

1. (18) The charge to fight the good fight.

This charge I commit to you, son Timothy, according to the prophecies previously made concerning you, that by them you may wage the good warfare.

a. **This charge I commit to you**: Again, the Greek word for **charge** (*parangelia*) is the same as in 1 Timothy 1:3; it is a military word, referring to an order from a commanding officer.

i. At the same time the words **son Timothy** express a note of fatherly love. Paul was serious, but full of love. "There is a peculiar affectionate earnestness in this use of the personal name, here and in the conclusion of the letter" (White).

b. **According to the prophecies**: Paul wanted Timothy to consider what the Holy Spirit had said to him through others in the past, and receive the courage to remain in Ephesus from those.

i. Apparently, God had spoken to Timothy through others through the gift of prophecy and the words were an encouragement for Timothy to stay strong in the difficulty right in front of him. It may have been a description of Timothy's future ministry; it may have been a warning against being timid in his work for God. Whatever it was, God wanted Timothy to draw strength from it in his present difficulty.

ii. So, the **prophecies** Timothy had received before might have been predictive of his future ministry, or may have not been. *He who prophesies speaks edification and exhortation and comfort to men* (1 Corinthians

14:3). It may or may not be presented as an announcement of the future.

iii. We shouldn't think it strange that God would speak to us through others in a prophetic manner; but we must take care to test all prophesy (1 Corinthians 14:29) according to both the Word of God and the witness of the Holy Spirit in others.

iv. We must also be on guard against the extravagant prophecy; the one that declares that this person or that is going to have "the most powerful ministry the world has seen" or such. These prophecies are extremely manipulative, because they are awkward to speak against.

v. Today, in some circles, it isn't unusual to hear someone being declared as greater than Paul, Peter, Moses, or Elijah; declarations like "You will be a prophet like unto Daniel and receive an anointing ten times greater than any of your associates" are obviously extravagant and manipulative (because few will speak against it). These are rarely from God.

iii. Tom Stipe, in the foreword to *Counterfeit Revival,* wrote powerfully about this phenomenon, having been a leader in such circles before seeing the wrong in it all:

After only a couple of years, the prophets seemed to be speaking to just about everyone on just about everything. Hundreds of... members received the 'gift' of prophecy and began plying their trade among both leaders and parishioners. People began carrying around little notebooks filled with predictions that had been delivered to them by the prophets and seers. They flocked to the prophecy conferences that had begun to spring up everywhere. The notebook crowd would rush forward in hopes of being selected to receive more prophecies to add to their prophetic diaries...

Not long after 'prophecy du jour' became the primary source of direction, a trail of devastated believers began to line up outside our pastoral counseling offices. Young people promised teen success and stardom through prophecy were left picking up the pieces of their shattered hopes because God had apparently gone back on His promises. Leaders were deluged by angry church members who had received prophecies about the great ministries they would have but had been frustrated by local church leaders who failed to recognize and 'facilitate' their 'new anointing.'

After a steady diet of the prophetic, some people were rapidly becoming biblically illiterate, choosing a 'dial-a-prophet' style of

Christian living rather than studying God's Word. Many were left to continually live from one prophetic 'fix' to the next, their hope always in danger of failing because God's voice was so specific in pronouncement, yet so elusive in fulfillment. Possessing a prophet's phone number was like having a storehouse of treasured guidance. Little clutched notebooks replaced Bibles as the preferred reading material during church services.

c. **That by them you may wage the good warfare**: The focus is not the prophetic word Timothy heard in the past. The focus is on battle right in front of him now, where he must **wage the good warfare** - that is, "fight the good fight" (KJV).

i. Timothy had a job in front of him, and it was going to be a battle. It wasn't going to be easy, or comfortable, or carefree. He had to approach the job Paul left him to do in Ephesus as a soldier approaches battle.

ii. This gave Timothy still another reason to remain in Ephesus. He should sense a responsibility to stay when he felt like leaving because he was like a soldier in a battle, who could not desert his post.

2. (19) Tools for the warfare: **faith and a good conscience**.

Having faith and a good conscience, which some having rejected, concerning the faith have suffered shipwreck.

a. **Faith and a good conscience**: These are essential when battling for the Lord. They protect against the spiritual attacks of doubt and condemnation.

i. Timothy had to have the **faith** that God was in control, and would guide him as Timothy continued to seek him.

ii. He had to have **a good conscience**, because his enemies would be attacking him, and if Timothy had not conducted himself rightly, they would have good reason to attack. A **good conscience** isn't just a conscience that approves us, but one that approves us because we've been doing what is right – it is connected with good conduct.

b. **Which some having rejected**: Some have **rejected** these weapons; specifically, Paul speaks of rejecting **the faith**; those who reject what Jesus and the apostles taught are headed for ruin (**shipwreck**).

i. **Which some having rejected**: "Having *thrust away*, as a fool-hardy soldier might his *shield* and his *breastplate* or a made sailor pilot, helm, and compass" (Clarke).

ii. "We are not justified in interpreting *suffered shipwreck* as though it meant that they were lost beyond hope of recovery. St. Paul himself had suffered shipwreck at least four times (2 Corinthians 11:25) when he wrote this epistle. He had on each occasion lost everything except himself." (White)

3. (20) Two people that rejected the tools for warfare.

Of whom are Hymenaeus and Alexander, whom I delivered to Satan that they may learn not to blaspheme.

a. **Of whom are Hymenaeus and Alexander**: We know nothing of **Hymenaeus and Alexander** other than what Paul said of them here. Paul apparently disciplined them for their disobedience to God in heresy, in conduct, or in both.

i. We see that Paul was not afraid to point out opponents of the truth by name, as he said to do in Romans 16:17. This was not a contradiction of Jesus' command not to judge (Matthew 7:1-5) "While Christians are not to judge one another's motives or ministries, we are certainly expected to be honest about each other's conduct" (Wiersbe).

b. **Whom I delivered to Satan**: From other New Testament passages we can surmise that he did this by putting them outside the church, into the world, which is the devil's domain. The punishment was a removal of protection, not an infliction of evil.

i. The Lord protects us from many attacks from Satan (Job 1:10; Luke 22:31-32), and much of this protection comes to us in what we receive as we gather together as Christians.

ii. In this, Paul gave Timothy one more reason to remain in Ephesus. He should do it because *not everyone else does*. We can't simply act as if every Christian does what God wants them to and stays faithful to the gospel. The fact that some do not remain faithful to the end should give us more incentive to not give up.

1 Timothy 2 - Instructions for Public Worship

A. Public prayer.

1. (1) Pray for all men.

Therefore I exhort first of all that supplications, prayers, intercessions, *and* giving of thanks be made for all men.

> a. **First of all**: This does not refer to time; it refers to importance. What comes next is of **first** importance in the heart and mind of Paul. Paul's broader context following is the public worship of Christians, so this begins a series of instructions for those meetings.
>
> > i. White translates the idea: "In the first place, let me remind you that the Church's public prayers must be made expressly for all men, from the Emperor downwards."
>
> b. **Supplications, prayers, intercessions, and giving of thanks**: These terms describe the wide categories of our communication with God. These are the kinds of prayer that should be offered when God's people come together.
>
> > i. **Supplication** is simply *asking* for something. Prayer should never be all asking, but it *should* ask in bold confidence from God's Word.
> >
> > ii. **Prayers** is a broad word, referring to all communication with the Lord.
> >
> > iii. **Intercessions** refer to the requests we make on behalf of others. As we pray, there should be time when the needs of other find a place in our prayer before God's throne.
> >
> > iv. **Giving of thanks** is an essential part of our walk with God. Those who lack a basic sense of gratitude in their lives lack a basic Christian virtue.

c. **All men**: This tells us *whom* we are to pray for with these various means of prayer. The idea is that **all men** need prayer. You have never met someone that you cannot or should not pray for.

i. Most Christians find it easy to pray for their family, friends, and loved ones, but it should not end there. We should also pray for our *enemies* and for those with whom we have conflict. We should pray for those who annoy us, and for those who seem to be against us. Each of these fall into the category of **all men**.

ii. To pray for **all men** also means to pray *evangelistically*. We should pray for our friends who need to know Jesus, for our coworkers, and for others we have regular contact with.

iii. To pray for **all men** also means to pray for your pastors, to pray for your church, and to pray for other ministries you know and love.

d. **Giving of thanks be made for all men**: We can find something to thank God for regarding **all men**. Even those who persecute us and are against us have a place in the over-arching plan of God.

2. (2) Pray for those in authority.

For kings and all who are in authority, that we may lead a quiet and peaceable life in all godliness and reverence.

a. **For kings and all who are in authority**: Early Christians were often accused of undermining the state because they claimed a higher Lord other than Caesar. Yet they would point out that they supported the state by being good citizens and by praying *for* the emperor, not *to* him.

i. In the previous verse Paul said that we should *give thanks* for all men, and here he connects the thought with those who are in authority over us. We should give thanks for those who are in authority, because God has ordained government in society to keep order (Romans 13:1-7).

ii. The early church leader Tertullian explained: "We pray for all the emperors, that God may grant them long life, a secure government, a prosperous family, vigorous troops, a faithful senate, an obedient people; that the whole world may be in peace; and that God may grant, both to Caesar and to every man, the accomplishment of their just desires." (Clarke)

b. **That we may lead a quiet and peaceable life in all godliness and reverence**: We should pray for a government and rulers that would simply leave us alone and let us live as Christians.

i. Christians are to look for no special favors from the government. Our goal is a level playing field, unrestricted by state intervention.

ii. At the time Paul wrote this, Christianity was not yet an illegal religion in the Roman Empire and it was still considered a branch of Judaism. It was even more reasonable to believe that the Roman government might just leave Christians alone to live their faith.

3. (3-4) The goal of prayer for all men: That they would be saved.

For this *is* good and acceptable in the sight of God our Savior, who desires all men to be saved and to come to the knowledge of the truth.

a. **Who desires all men to be saved**: Prayer for those in authority should always have an evangelical purpose. Our real goal is that they would come under the authority of Jesus, and make decisions allowing the gospel to have free course and be glorified.

b. **Who desires all men to be saved**: On a human level, we can certainly say that God **desires all men to be saved**. There is no one in such high authority that they don't need salvation in Jesus.

i. However, from a divine perspective, we understand there is a sense in which we can *not* say that God **desires all men to be saved** - otherwise, either all men would automatically *be saved*, or God would not have left an element of human response in the gospel.

ii. God's desire for all men to be saved is conditioned by His desire to have a genuine response from human beings. He won't fulfill His desire to save all men at the expense of making men robots that worship Him from simply being programmed to do so.

c. **Who desires all men to be saved**: Because this is true (as seen from a human perspective), therefore the gospel must be presented to all without reservation. Any idea of limiting evangelism to the elect is absurd.

d. **All men to be saved and to come to the knowledge of the truth**: Salvation is clearly associated with coming **to the knowledge of the truth**. One cannot be saved apart from at least some understanding of who Jesus is and what He has done to save us.

4. (5-7) How all men must be saved.

For *there is* one God and one Mediator between God and men, *the* Man Christ Jesus, who gave Himself a ransom for all, to be testified in due time, for which I was appointed a preacher and an apostle; I am speaking the truth in Christ *and* not lying; a teacher of the Gentiles in faith and truth.

a. **One God and one Mediator**: Through one Mediator, and One alone: **The Man Christ Jesus**. There is no valid way to God that does not come through Jesus.

i. This statement of Paul simply echoes what Jesus said in John 14:6: *Jesus said to him, "I am the way, the truth, and the life. No one comes to the Father except through Me."*

ii. It is also simply logical. If Jesus was at least a good and honest man, then He told the truth when He said that He was the only way to God. If He did not tell the truth at this important point, then it is difficult to regard His as even a good or honest man, much less a prophet from God. If He was wrong then He was either a liar or a lunatic.

iii. In the modern world most people think that any road leads to God, *if followed sincerely* or *with a good heart*. The Bible argues against this idea.

- The Pharisee and the tax collector each came to God sincerely, but one was accepted, and one was not (Luke 18:9-14).

- The rich young ruler came to Jesus sincerely, but was rejected because he did not give up everything to follow Jesus (Luke 18:18-23).

- In Leviticus 10:1-3, the story of Nadab and Abihu – and God's judgment upon them – makes it clear that we cannot come to God any way we please, and that sincerity is not enough.

- Proverbs 14:12 is instructive: *There is a way that seems right to a man, but its end is the way of death.*

iv. Many people think that God would be unfair or narrow minded to have only one way to salvation; but the thought needs to be turned over. To say that God is unfair for this, one would have to look at Jesus dying on the cross – the spotless Son of God, came from heaven and lived humbly and died in horrific agony, both physical and spiritual – to look at Jesus on the cross and say, "Thanks God; I appreciate the gesture, but that *isn't enough.* You're going to have to do a little more than that, because that is only *one way* and if You are fair You will make *several ways."*

b. **The Man Christ Jesus**: This reminds us that Jesus is still human, even as He is enthroned in heaven right now. His humanity was not merely a temporary phase. When the Eternal Son, the Second Person of the Trinity, added humanity to His deity, He added it forever – not only for 33 years.

i. Jesus is still fully God and fully man, but His humanity is glorified and resurrected. It is the pattern of the humanity that we will experience in heaven.

c. **Who gave Himself**: Jesus gave **Himself**. You can give your time without giving yourself. You can give your money without giving yourself. You can give your opinion without giving yourself. You can even give your life without giving yourself. Jesus wants us to give ourselves, just as He **gave Himself**.

d. **Who gave Himself a ransom**: Jesus gave Himself as a *hostage*, as a payment for our sins. He put Himself in our place and received the punishment and wrath from God the Father that we deserved. This is the basic message of the gospel.

i. **A ransom for all**: There is enough in the work of Jesus on the cross for everyone. No one will be turned away because Jesus ran out of love or forgiveness at the cross for them.

e. **For which I was appointed a preacher and an apostle**: This was the message Paul preached. The message was of salvation only through Jesus, and Jesus crucified (as in 1 Corinthians 2:1-2).

f. **A teacher of the Gentiles**: Paul began his ministry with an equal emphasis to both Jew and Gentile (Acts 13), but because of continued rejection by Jews, Paul began to emphasize his ministry to the Gentiles.

B. Men and women in the church.

1. (8) The role of men in leading prayer when the church gathers.

I desire therefore that the men pray everywhere, lifting up holy hands, without wrath and doubting.

a. **That the men pray everywhere**: This has the idea of "In every church," and not of "In every place." Paul's focus is on what the church does when it comes together for meetings.

i. The idea that we should pray constantly and that prayer should be a normal part of our live wherever we go is good and valid; but it is not what Paul means here.

ii. White on **everywhere**: "The directions are to apply to every Church without exception; no allowance is to be made for the conditions peculiar to any locality."

b. **That the men**: Makes it clear Paul assumed **men** would take the lead at meetings of the congregation. Since the lifting up of hands was a common posture of prayer in ancient cultures, this text speaks of men leading public prayer - men representing the congregation before God's throne.

i. White translates the idea of the text: "The ministers of public prayer must be the men of the congregation, not the women."

c. **Lifting up holy hands**: Hands that are lifted up must be **holy** – hands that are set apart unto God, and not given over to evil.

d. **Without wrath and doubting**: Such prayers must be **without wrath** (praying "angry" prayers) and without **doubting** (praying without faith). When we pray angry, or pray without faith, we can do more bad than good – especially when the prayer is public.

i. "Having no vindictive feeling against any person; harboring no unforgiving spirit, while they are imploring pardon for their own offences." (Clarke)

2. (9-10) Women should emphasize *spiritual* preparation and beauty more than *physical* preparation and beauty.

In like manner also, that the women adorn themselves in modest apparel, with propriety and moderation, not with braided hair or gold or pearls or costly clothing, but, which is proper for women professing godliness, with good works.

a. **In like manner also**: The word **also** refers back to the statement *that the men pray everywhere* in 1 Timothy 2:8. Paul thought the principle of 1 Timothy 2:8 should apply in various congregations, and so should the principle in 1 Timothy 2:9.

b. **That the women adorn themselves in modest apparel**: This is how Christian women are supposed to dress, especially at their Christian meetings. The words **propriety and moderation** help explain what **modest apparel** is.

i. **Propriety** asks, "Is it appropriate for the occasion? Is it over-dressed or under-dressed? Is it going to call inappropriate attention to myself?" **Moderation** asks, "Is it moderate? Is it just too much – or far too little?" **Moderation** looks for a middle ground.

ii. The **braided hair or gold or pearls or costly clothing** Paul mentions were adornments that went against the principles of **propriety** and **moderation** in that culture.

iii. How you dress reflects your heart. If a man dresses in a casual manner, it says something about his attitude. Likewise, if a woman dresses in an immodest manner, it says something about her heart.

iv. "Woman has been invidiously defined: *An animal fond of dress.* How long will they permit themselves to be thus degraded?" (Clarke)

c. **But... with good works**: The most important adornment is **good works**. If a woman is dressed in propriety and moderation, with good works, she is perfectly dressed. **Good works** make a woman more beautiful than good jewelry.

3. (11-12) Women are to show submission, and yield to the authority of the men God has appointed to lead in the church.

Let a woman learn in silence with all submission. And I do not permit a woman to teach or to have authority over a man, but to be in silence.

a. **Let a woman learn in silence**: This unfortunate translation has led some to believe that it is forbidden for women to even speak in church meetings. Paul uses the same word translated **silence** in 1 Timothy 2:2, and it is translated *peaceable* there. The idea is *without contention* instead of total silence.

> i. In other places in the New Testament, even in the writings of Paul, women are specifically mentioned as praying and speaking in the church (1 Corinthians 11:5). To **learn in silence** has the idea of women receiving the teaching of the men God has chosen to lead in the church, with **submission** instead of *contention*.

> ii. **Submission** is the principle; to **learn in silence** describes the application of the principle.

> iii. Some have said the reason for this is because in these ancient cultures (as well as some present-day cultures), men and women sat in separate sections. The thought is that women interrupted the church service by shouting questions and comments to their husbands during the service. Clarke expresses this idea: "It was lawful for *men* in public assemblies to ask questions, or even interrupt the speaker when there was any matter in his speech which they did not understand; but this liberty was not granted to *women*."

b. **With all submission**: The word for **submission** here literally means, "To be under in rank." It has to do with respecting an acknowledged order of authority. It certainly does not mean that men are more spiritual than women or that women are inferior to men.

> i. "Anyone who has served in the armed forces knows that 'rank' has to do with order and authority, not with value or ability… Just as an army would be in confusion if there were no levels of authority, so society would be in chaos without submission." (Wiersbe)

c. **I do not permit a woman to teach or to have authority over a man**: Paul's meaning seems clear. Women are not to have the role of teaching authority in the church. To be *under authority* is the principle; *not teaching* is the application.

i. Paul is saying that the church should not recognize women as those having authority in the church regarding matters of doctrine and Scriptural interpretation.

ii. Not all speaking or teaching by a woman is *necessarily* a violation of God's order of authority in the church. Whatever speaking or teaching is done by a woman must be done in submission to the men God has appointed to lead the church.

iii. 1 Corinthians 11:1-12 emphasizes the same principle. Women are to always act *under authority* in the congregation, demonstrated in Corinthian culture by the wearing of a head covering. Therefore a woman in the Corinthian church could only pray or prophesy if she demonstrated that she was under the leadership of the church, and she demonstrated this by wearing a head covering and by acting consistently with that principle.

d. **I do not permit**: The strength of Paul's wording here makes it challenging to obey this command in today's society. Since the 1970's, our culture has rejected the idea that there may be different roles for men and women in the home, in the professional world, or in the church. In this text (among others), the Holy Spirit clearly says there *is* a difference in roles.

i. But the cultural challenge must be seen in its true context - not just a struggle between men and women, but as a struggle with the issue of authority in general. Since the 1960's, there has been a massive change in the way we see and accept authority.

- Citizens do not have the same respect for government's authority.
- Students do not have the same respect for teacher's authority.
- Women do not have the same respect for men's authority.
- Children do not have the same respect for parental authority.
- Employees do not have the same respect for their employer's authority.
- People do not have the same respect for the police's authority.
- Christians no longer have the same respect for church authority.

ii. There are not many who would say that these changes have been *good*. Generally, people do not feel safer and there is less confidence in the culture. Television and other entertainment get worse and worse. In fact, our society is presently in, and rushing towards, complete anarchy - the state where no authority is accepted, and the only thing that matters is what one *wants* to do.

iii. It is fair to describe our present moral state as one of anarchy. There is no moral authority in our culture. When it comes to morality, the only thing that matters is what one wants to do. And in a civil sense, many neighborhoods in our nation are given over to anarchy. The government's authority is not accepted in gang-infested portions of our cities. The only thing that matters is what one *wants* to do.

iv. We must see the broader attack on authority as a direct Satanic strategy to destroy our society and millions of individual lives. He is accomplishing this with two main attacks. First, the *corruption* of authority; second, the *rejection* of authority.

v. This idea of authority and submission to authority are so important to God that they are part of His very being. The First Person of the Holy Trinity is called the *Father*; the Second Person of the Holy Trinity is called the *Son*. Inherent in those titles is a relationship of authority and submission to authority. The Father exercises authority over the Son, and the Son submits to the Father's authority - and this is in the *very nature and being* of God. Our failure to exercise Biblical authority, and our failure to submit to Biblical authority, isn't just wrong and sad - it sins against the very nature of God. 1 Samuel 15:23 speaks to this same principle: *For rebellion is as the sin of witchcraft.*

e. **I do not permit a woman to teach or to have authority over a man**: Paul's focus here is the public worship of the church. God has established a clear chain of authority in both the home and in the church, and in those spheres, God has ordained that men are the "head" - that is, that they have the place of authority and responsibility.

i. Our culture, having rejected the idea in a difference in *role* between men and women, now rejects the idea of *any_difference* between men and women. The driving trends in our culture point towards men who are more like women, and women who are more like men. Styles, clothes, perfumes, and all the rest promote this thought.

ii. The Bible is just as specific that there is no *general* submission of women unto men commanded in society; only in the spheres of the home and in the church. God has not commanded in His word that men have exclusive authority in the areas of politics, business, education, and so on.

iii. It also does not mean that *every* woman in the church is under the authority of *every* man in the church. Instead it means that those who lead the church - pastors and ruling elders - must be men, and the women (and others) must respect their authority.

iv. The failure of men to lead in the home and in the church, and to lead in the way Jesus would lead, has been a chief cause of the rejection of male authority - and is inexcusable.

v. Some feel this recognition and submission to authority is an unbearable burden. They feel that it means, "I have to say that I am inferior, that I am nothing, and I have to recognize this other person as being superior." Yet inferiority or superiority has nothing to do with this. We remember the relationship between God the Father and God the Son - they are completely equal in their being, but have different roles when it comes to authority.

vi. Some may say that the church cannot work (or cannot work *well*) unless we go along with the times and put women into positions of spiritual and doctrinal authority in the church. From the standpoint of what works in our culture, they may be right. Yet from the standpoint of pleasing God by doing what He says in His word, they are wrong.

4. (13-14) Reasons for God's recognition of male authority in the church.

For Adam was formed first, then Eve. And Adam was not deceived, but the woman being deceived, fell into transgression.

a. **For Adam was formed first**: The first reason for male authority in the church is order of creation. Adam (man) was created first, and given original authority on earth.

i. The first command God gave to the human race is found in Genesis 2:16-17: *Of every tree of the garden you may freely eat; but of the tree of the knowledge of good and evil you shall not eat, for in the day that you eat of it you shall surely die.* This command was not given to woman at all. At the time that command was given, Eve was not yet created from Adam.

ii. Therefore, Adam received his command and his authority from God, and Eve received her command and authority from Adam.

b. **The woman being deceived**: The second reason is the difference in the sin of Adam and Eve, as connected to their difference in authority.

i. Both Adam and Eve sinned in the Garden of Eden, and Eve clearly sinned first. Yet, the Bible never blames Eve for the fall of the human race, but always blames Adam (*through one man sin entered the world*, Romans 5:12). Adam is responsible because of there was a difference of authority. Adam had an authority Eve did not have; therefore he also had a *responsibility* Eve did not have. Adam failed in his responsibility in a far more significant way than Eve did.

ii. As well, Eve was **deceived**, and Adam **was not deceived**. Eve was tricked; but Adam sinned knew exactly what he was doing when he rebelled. This means that though Adam's sin was worse, Eve's ability to be more readily deceived made her more dangerous in a place of authority. "Eve's reasoning faculty was at once overcome by the allegation of jealousy felt by God, an allegation plausible to a nature swayed by emotion rather than by reflection." (White)

iii. Generally speaking, it may be observed that women seem to be more spiritually sensitive than men - but this can be true for good or evil.

iv. **Adam... the woman**: "St. Paul says *woman* rather than *Eve*, emphasizing the sex rather than the individual, because he desires to give the incident its general application, especially in view of what follows." (White)

v. Significantly, these reasons are not dependent upon culture. Those who say "Paul was a sexist man in a sexist culture," and discount these words, are simply not reading what the Holy Spirit says in the sacred Scriptures here.

5. (15) Being a Christian woman in light of Eve's curse.

Nevertheless she will be saved in childbearing if they continue in faith, love, and holiness, with self-control.

a. **Nevertheless she will be saved in childbearing**: Many people regard this as one of the most difficult passages in the whole Bible. On the surface, it could be taken to mean that if a woman continues in faith, love, and holiness, with self-control, that God will bless her with survival in childbirth – which was no small promise in the ancient world.

i. Yet this interpretation leaves many difficult questions. Is this an absolute promise? What about godly women who have died in childbirth? What about sinful women who have survived childbirth? Doesn't this seem like just a reward for good works, and not according to God's grace and mercy?

b. **Saved in childbearing if they continue in faith, love, and holiness, with self control**: Some approach this passage saying **saved** refers to gaining eternal life. Yet this interpretation is even more difficult. Are women saved eternally by giving birth to children - but only if they continue with godly virtues? What about women who *can't* have children? Are they denied salvation?

c. **She will be saved in childbearing**: Some say that Paul "Has mostly in mind that child-bearing, not public teaching, is the peculiar function of woman, with a glory and dignity all its own." (Robinson) The idea is that one should let the men teach in church and let the women have the babies.

d. **She will be saved in childbearing**: A better way to approach this passage is based on the grammar in the original Greek language. In the original, it says *she will be saved in <u>the childbirth</u>*. This has the sense, "Even though women were deceived, and fell into transgression starting with Eve, women can be saved by the Messiah - whom a woman brought into the world."

> i. Probably, the idea here is that even though the "woman race" did something bad in the garden by being deceived and falling into transgression, the "woman race" also did something far greater, in being used by God to bring the saving Messiah into the world.

> ii. The summary is this: Don't blame women for the fall of the human race; the Bible doesn't. Instead, thank women for bringing the Messiah to us.

e. **Faith, love, and holiness, with self-control**: Most of all, we should note these positives. They are all qualities God wants to be evident in women, and that women have effectively nurtured in their children through generations.

1 Timothy 3 - Qualifications for Leaders

A. Qualifications for a bishop.

1. (1) Introduction the good work of spiritual leadership.

This *is* a faithful saying: If a man desires the position of a bishop, he desires a good work.

a. **This is a faithful saying**: Paul has just written that women are not to hold positions of spiritual or doctrinal authority over congregations, but he did not want to leave the impression that just *any* man is qualified. No man is qualified to be a spiritual leader in the church just because of his gender.

b. **If a man desires the position of a bishop**: The office Paul described is that of **bishop**. Our religious culture has given us a particular idea of what a **bishop** is; but the word **bishop** in New Testament Greek [*episkopos*] literally means "over" (*epi*) "watcher" (*skopos*) – an *overseer*.

i. These were men with leadership and authority in the church. "The *state* has its *monarch*, the *Church* has its *bishop*; one should govern according to the *laws of the land*, the other according to the *word of God*" (Clarke).

ii. In Acts 20:17, we learn there were several *bishops* – that is, overseers – in one church in one city. Undoubtedly, these were men who had oversight over the many house-churches that met throughout the city.

iii. Based on what **bishop** means, a bishop is someone with *oversight* in the church, a leader. Such a person may also sometimes be called an *elder* (*presbuteros*) or a *pastor* (*poimen*, which means "shepherd"), as in Acts 20:17 and 20:28.

iv. "On the question as to the terms presbyter and episcopus, it is sufficient here to state my own conclusion, that they represent slightly different aspects of the same office, pastoral and official; aspects which came naturally into prominence in the Jewish and Greek societies respectively which gave birth to the names." (White)

v. Of this passage, White adds: "Having given elementary directions concerning the scope of public prayer, and the ministers thereof, St. Paul now takes up the matter of Church organization." Yet this organization of the church is greatly limited. There is no advice or guidance on structure or exactly how the offices of **bishop** or deacon or anything else relate to each other. In the New Testament design, there seems to be some flexibility on *structure* and an emphasis rather on the *character* of leaders.

c. **He desires a good work**: The idea isn't, "Good for you, you want to have a place of spiritual leadership," even though that can be a godly desire. The idea is more like this: "This is a good, noble, honorable work. Timothy, you need to look for good, noble, honorable men."

i. "For it is no light matter to represent God's Son in such a great task as erecting and extending God's kingdom, in caring for the salvation of souls whom the Lord Himself has deigned to purchase with His own blood, and ruling the Church which is God's inheritance." (Calvin)

d. **He desires a good work**: Spiritual leadership in the church isn't all about titles and honor and glory; it's about **work**. Jesus said: *If anyone desires to be first, he shall be last of all and servant of all* (Mark 9:35).

i. "*A good work*, But a hard work. The ministry is not an idle man's occupation, but a sore labour." (Trapp)

ii. "What is the use of a lazy minister? He is no good either to the world, to the Church, or to himself. He is a dishonor to the noblest profession that can be bestowed upon the sons of men." (Spurgeon)

2. (2a) Qualifications for bishops.

A bishop then must be…

a. **A bishop then must be**: God has specific *qualifications* for leaders in the church. Leaders are not to be chosen at random, nor just because they volunteer, nor because they aspire to the position, nor even because they are "natural leaders." Instead they should be chosen primarily on how they match the qualifications listed here.

i. The qualifications for leadership have nothing to do with *giftedness*. God doesn't say, "Go out and get the most gifted men." God may easily and instantly create gifts in a man, because gifts are given by the Holy Spirit as He wills (1 Corinthians 12:11).

ii. Going to seminary doesn't make one qualified for spiritual leadership. Being a good talker doesn't make one qualified for spiritual leadership. Natural or spiritual gifts in themselves do not qualify one for spiritual leadership. What one gives in money or volunteer time does not qualify them for spiritual leadership. What qualifies a man for spiritual leadership is *godly character* - and godly character established according to these clear criteria.

b. **Then must be**: However, this is not a rigid list which demands *perfection* in all areas; they are both goals to reach for and general criteria for selection. When looking for church leaders, one should look at this list and ask:

- Does the man in question desire all these things with his whole heart?
- Does that desire show itself in his life?
- Are there others available who better fulfill the requirements of this list?

c. **Must be**: As well, these qualifications are valuable for every person, and not only those who aspire to leadership. They are clear indicators of godly character and spiritual maturity and they can give a true measure of a man.

3. (2b-7) A list of qualifications for leaders in the church.

Blameless, the husband of one wife, temperate, sober-minded, of good behavior, hospitable, able to teach; not given to wine, not violent, not greedy for money, but gentle, not quarrelsome, not covetous; one who rules his own house well, having *his* children in submission with all reverence (for if a man does not know how to rule his own house, how will he take care of the church of God?); not a novice, lest being puffed up with pride he fall into the *same* condemnation as the devil. Moreover he must have a good testimony among those who are outside, lest he fall into reproach and the snare of the devil.

a. **Blameless**: This word literally means, "Nothing to take hold upon." There must be nothing in his life that others can take hold of and attack the church.

i. "The word is a metaphor, taken from the case of an expert and skilful pugilist, who *so defends every part of* his *body* that it is impossible for his antagonist to give one hit." (Clarke)

ii. This is a broad term for a man who lives a righteous life that can be *seen* as righteous. No one can stand up and rightfully accuse the man of grievous sin.

iii. In 1 Timothy 3:10, in speaking about deacons, Paul used the phrase *being found blameless*. This implies being *blameless* is demonstrated by a track record of behavior.

b. **Husband of one wife**: The idea here is of "A one-woman man." It is not that a leader *must* be married (if so, then both Jesus and Paul could not be spiritual leaders in our churches). Nor is the idea that leader could never remarry if his wife had passed away or was Biblically divorced. The idea is that is love and affection and heart is given to **one** woman, and that being his lawful and wedded wife.

i. This means that the Biblical leader is not a playboy, an adulterer, a flirt, and does not show romantic or sexual interest in other women, including the depictions or images of women in pornography.

c. **Temperate**: The idea is of someone who is *not given to extremes*. They are reliable and trustworthy, and you don't have to worry about wide swings of vision, mood, or action.

d. **Soberminded**: This describes the person who is *able to think clearly and with clarity*. They are not constantly joking but know how to deal with serious subjects in a serious way.

i. "This does not man he has no sense of humor, or that he is always solemn and somber. Rather it suggests that he knows the value of things and does not cheapen the ministry or the Gospel message by foolish behavior." (Wiersbe)

e. **Of good behavior**: The idea is "orderly." It is the same word translated *modest* in 1 Timothy 2:9. "*Orderly*, perhaps *dignified* in the best sense of the term" (White).

f. **Hospitable**: They are willing and able to open up their home to both friends and strangers.

g. **Able to teach**: This means they are skilled enough in the Bible to teach, either in a public or one-on-one setting.

h. **Not given to wine**: The idea is of not being addicted to wine or intoxicating drink. This verse, in itself, does not *prohibit* godly leadership from drinking alcoholic beverages, but it clearly discourages it.

i. "No ale-stake, tavern-haunter, that sits close at it, till the wine inflame him." (Trapp)

i. **Not violent**: This is a man who is not given to violence either publicly nor privately; a man who can let God fight his cause.

j. **Not greedy for money**: The King James Versions puts it far more memorably: *not greedy of filthy lucre*.

i. "I repeat that the man who will not bear poverty patiently and willingly will inevitably become the victim of mean and sordid covetousness." (Calvin)

k. **Gentle**: The kind of man who takes Jesus as his example, not the latest action hero.

l. **Not quarrelsome**: The kind of person who is not always fighting over something or other.

m. **Not covetous**: This is a more encompassing thought than merely *greedy for money*. The **covetous** man is never satisfied with anything, always demanding something more or different. A man who is constantly *dissatisfied* is not fit for leadership among God's people.

n. **Who rules his own house well**: The godly leader demonstrates his leadership ability first in his own home; Paul recognized that it is in the home where our Christianity is first demonstrated.

i. It is true that a child may rebel from even a good home; but is the rebellion *because* of the parents or *in spite* of their job as parents? This is the question that must be asked.

o. **Not a novice**: New converts should not be given leadership too quickly. The leader should be well past the **novice** stage in their spiritual development.

i. **Novice** is literally "newly planted." When someone first comes to Jesus, it isn't good to put them into a place of leadership until they have been allowed to grow long enough to put down some deep roots.

ii. "Novices are not only bold and impetuous, but are puffed up with foolish self-confidence, as though they could fly beyond the clouds" (Calvin). Promoting a novice too quickly gives occasion to the great sin - pride, in imitation of the Devil himself.

p. **A good testimony**: These characteristics must be evident to all, even unbelievers to see. The potential leader must be a good Christian *outside* the walls of the church.

B. Qualifications for deacons.

1. (8a) **Deacons**, the practical servants of the church.

Likewise deacons *must be...*

a. **Likewise deacons**: An example of the appointment of deacons is in Acts 6:1-6, where the apostles saw the need for those to distribute the daily assistance to the widows among the church yet did not have the time to distribute the aid themselves. They chose men to act essentially as deacons in that church.

b. **Deacons must be**: Their qualifications are much the same as those for "bishops"; practical service (especially when recognized by an office) is leadership also.

> i. It is a mistake to see one office as more prestigious than the other, though bishops have more responsibility before God. Each is more a matter of *calling* than status.

2. (8b-12) Qualifications for deacons.

Reverent, not double-tongued, not given to much wine, not greedy for money, holding the mystery of the faith with a pure conscience. But let these also first be tested; then let them serve as deacons, being *found* blameless. Likewise *their* wives *must be* reverent, not slanderers, temperate, faithful in all things. Let deacons be the husbands of one wife, ruling *their* children and their own houses well.

a. **Reverent**: Showing proper respect towards both God and man.

b. **Not double-tongued**: A man who speaks the truth the first time, with no intent to deceive.

c. **Holding the mystery of the faith**: Those who can adhere to proper doctrine, out of sincere conviction.

d. **First be proved**: A man *demonstrates* his fitness for office in the church by his conduct. Deacons and bishops are more *recognized* than *appointed*.

e. **Likewise their wives**: It is difficult to know if Paul here referred here to female deacons (such as Phoebe, in Romans 16:1), or the wives of male deacons. The original wording will permit either possibility.

> i. If he is speaking mainly of a male deacon's wife, it is appropriate because a man's leadership in the home can be evaluated, in part, by his wife's conduct. Is she **reverent, not** [one of the] **slanderers, temperate,** and **faithful in all things**?

> ii. **Not slanderers**: "Literally, *not devils*. This may be properly enough translated *slanderers, backbiters, tale-bearers,* for all these are of their father, the devil, and his lusts they will do" (Clarke).

3. (13) A promise for deacons.

For those who have served well as deacons obtain for themselves a good standing and great boldness in the faith which is in Christ Jesus.

a. **For those who have served well as deacons**: God remembers their faithful service, even in tasks which some would consider menial. There is little doubt that you will see more **deacons** with a great reward than bishops or pastors.

b. **The faith which is in Christ Jesus**: All the work of servant-leaders in God's family is pointed towards building among God's people **the faith which is in Christ Jesus**.

C. The mystery of godliness.

1. (14-15) Paul's reason for writing Timothy.

These things I write to you, though I hope to come to you shortly; but if I am delayed, *I write* so that you may know how you ought to conduct yourself in the house of God, which is the church of the living God, the pillar and ground of the truth.

a. **These things I write to you, though I hope to come to you shortly**: Paul desired to speak these things to Timothy personally, but knowing he might not be able to come as soon as he wished, Paul made certain that he said it in a letter.

   i. "This verse makes it clear that Timothy's position was a temporary one; he was acting as St. Paul's representative at Ephesus." (White)

b. **How you ought to conduct yourself in the house of God**: Paul's purpose for writing was to give Timothy, as a leader, practical information on how to run things in the Ephesian church.

c. **The house of God**: The church must be, very consciously, the place where God is. This makes a church more attractive than anything else.

   i. The Church is God's house because…

   • He is the Architect.
   • He is the Builder.
   • He lives there.
   • He provides for it.
   • He is honored there, and He rules there.

d. **The church of the living God**: In the ancient Greek language, "**church**" was a non-religious word for a group of people called together for a purpose. The **living God** has called His people together for His purpose.

e. **The pillar and ground of truth**: The pillar and ground (foundation) of the church is **truth**. Tragically, many churches today don't value the truth as they should and are therefore left weak pillars and shaky ground.

i. "The Church is the pillar of the truth because by its ministry the truth is preserved and spread… Paul will not acknowledge the Church except where God's truth is exalted and plain." (Calvin)

ii. It isn't that the church is the foundation *for* the truth, but that the church *holds up* the truth so the world can see it. "Pillars also were of ancient use to fasten upon them any public edicts, which princes or courts would have published, and exposed to the view of all; hence the church is called, *the pillar* and basis, or seal, *of truth*, because by it the truths of God are published, supported, and defended" (Poole).

iii. "When the Church stands boldly out, and preaches the Word, it is the pillar of the truth; when it is hidden in the Roman catacombs, and cannot proclaim the Savior's name to the world, still there lives the truth deep in the hearts of believers, and they are then the ground of the truth." (Spurgeon)

2. (16) An early hymn to express the foundation of Christian truth.

And without controversy great is the mystery of godliness:

God was manifested in the flesh,
Justified in the Spirit,
Seen by angels,
Preached among the Gentiles,
Believed on in the world,
Received up in glory.

a. **Without controversy**: The wonderful summary of Christian truth in 1 Timothy 3:16 *should* be **without controversy** among believers. It is unfortunate when those who claim to be Christians debate or deny these fundamental truths.

i. "When he says 'without controversy,' I suppose he means that there ought to be no controversy about these facts, though controversies have arisen concerning them, and always will, since the most self-evident truth will always find self-evident fools to contradict it." (Spurgeon)

b. **God was manifested in the flesh**: This is the essence of the incarnation; that God the Son, the Second Person of the Holy Trinity, added to His deity humanity - and was thus **manifested in the flesh**.

i. "Observe that the comprehensive summary of the gospel here given is contained in six little sentences, which run with such regularity of measure in the original Greek, that some have supposed them to be an ancient hymn; and it is possible that they may have been used as such in the early church." (Spurgeon)

c. **Justified in the Spirit**: We can say that Jesus was **justified by the Spirit** not in the sense that He was once sinful but made righteous, but in the sense that He was declared to be, by the Holy Spirit, what He always was - completely justified before the Father.

> i. This declaration was made at His baptism (Matthew 3:16), and at His resurrection (1 Peter 3:18; Acts 2:32-33).

d. **Seen by angels**: The ministry of Jesus, both on earth and through the Church, is of great interest to angelic beings. There were many instances when Jesus was seen by angels (Mark 1:13; Luke 22:41-43), and especially at the resurrection (Matthew 28:2-7).

> i. "The apostle mentions this to show the greatness of our religion, since the noblest intellects are interested in it. Did you ever hear of angels hovering around the assemblies of philosophical societies?" (Spurgeon)

> ii. "The Godhead was seen in Christ by angels, as they had never seen it before. They had beheld the attribute of justice, they had seen the attribute of power, they had marked the attribute of wisdom, and seen the Prerogative of sovereignty; but never had angels seen love, and condescension, and tenderness, and pity, in God as they saw these things resplendent in the person and the life of Christ." (Spurgeon)

e. **Preached among the Gentiles, believed on in the world**: Paul himself did his best to *fulfill* these statements. He was busy preaching Jesus among the Gentiles and bringing the world to belief.

> i. "God's way of creating faith in men's hearts is not by pictures, music, or symbols, but by the hearing of the word of God. This may seem a strange thing, and strange let it seem, for it is a mystery, and a great mystery, but a fact beyond all controversy; for ever let the church maintain that Christ is to be preached unto the Gentiles." (Spurgeon)

f. **Received up in glory**: This reminds us of Jesus' ascension (Luke 24:51), His finished work on our behalf (Hebrews 1:3), and His present intercession for us (1 John 2:1).

> i. "He was so received because his work is finished. He would never have gone into his glory if he had not finished all his toil. He would have accepted no reward had he not fully earned it." (Spurgeon)

> ii. **Received up in glory**: Jesus ascended into heaven in a resurrection body; yet it was a body that still retained the marks of His great work of love for us. It still had the nail prints in His hands and feet, the wound in his side, all marks of His suffering on our behalf (John 20:24-29).

iii. Paul's description of Jesus after the passage speaking of Christian character reminds us of the key to our own character transformation - beholding Jesus. It is just as Paul wrote in 2 Corinthians 3:18: *But we all, with unveiled face, beholding as in a mirror the glory of the Lord, are being transformed into the same image from glory to glory, just as by the Spirit of the Lord.*

iv. Jesus is the perfect fulfillment of these descriptions of Christian character. We trust that Jesus will transform our life according to the same character, as we put our focus on Him. We sometimes want *religion* to build this character in us; but truly, *relationship* with Jesus is what really does it.

1 Timothy 4 – God's Man of Truth and Integrity

A. False doctrine in the end times.

1. (1) A warning from the Holy Spirit.

Now the Spirit expressly says that in latter times some will depart from the faith, giving heed to deceiving spirits and doctrines of demons.

a. **Now the Spirit expressly says**: Paul especially marked this as a revelation from the Holy Spirit; either as a spontaneous word given as he wrote or quoting from a previous prophecy. Paul knew certain dangers would mark the **latter times**.

- The danger of *apostasy* (**some will depart**).
- The danger of *deception* (**deceiving spirits**).
- The danger of *false teaching* (**doctrines of demons**).

   i. It has been more than 1900 years since Paul wrote to Timothy about **the latter times**, but he did not misunderstand his time or our own. History is not, and has not, been rushing towards a distant brink that would end this current order; even in apostolic times, history had reached that brink - and has run parallel to it since. As it turns out, the **latter times** describe a broad era, not a couple of years.

b. **Some will depart from the faith**: Because of the danger of the latter times, if Timothy were to remain a faithful minister to God's people, he must keep a dead reckoning on the truth – **the faith**. If this were lost, not much else really mattered.

   i. "A man may hold all the truths of Christianity, and yet render them of none effect by holding other doctrines which counteract their influence; or he may apostatize by denying some essential doctrine, though he bring in nothing *heterodox*." (Clarke)

ii. A June 1997 article in U.S. News and World Report described a Virginia pastor who "Would rather preach on 'Bosnia, justice, or world peace' than on Bible stories or personal salvation." This is an example of a man who departed from the faith and followed his own direction.

c. **The faith**: This doesn't mean losing the ability to believe, but losing the content of what Christians should believe. It describes the essential teachings of the Christian faith. When **some... depart from the faith**, they are abandoning the essential teachings of Christianity.

i. The Bible uses the phrase "**the faith**" in this way many places: Acts 6:7 and 14:22, Colossians 1:23, 1 Timothy 1:19, and Jude 1:3.

d. **Deceiving spirits**: This refers to demonic spirits (angelic beings who have rebelled against God), who seek to deceive men and women and to entice them away from the truth.

i. Some lies are so powerful that they have an evident spiritual dynamic behind them. These are lies crafted and promoted by deceiving spirits.

e. **Doctrines of demons**: This speaks of the specific *teachings* of these **deceiving spirits**. Demons are theology majors, and have systems of doctrine.

i. We find the first demonic doctrine in Genesis 3. There Satan, speaking through a serpent, taught Eve: *You will not surely die. For God knows that in the day you eat of it your eyes will be opened, and you will be like God* (Genesis 3:4-5). Since then, every demonic doctrine has found its way back to this root: the idea that we can be gods, and operate independently from God.

ii. "Many MSS. and the chief of the fathers have... *spirits of deceit*; which is much more emphatic than the common reading. Deception has her spirits, emissaries of every kind, which she employs to darken the hearts and destroy the souls of men. Pretenders to *inspiration*, and false teachers of every kind, belong to this class." (Clarke)

f. **Deceiving spirits... doctrines of demons**: These have been around since man first walked the Garden of Eden. But we should expect that more and more people in the church would **depart from the faith** in the latter times and accept these false teachings.

i. It is hard to say if there is more false teaching today, or if it is merely a case of modern technology being able to spread the lie better. But the old saying is certainly true today: a lie travels at top speed while the truth goes on foot – and more people within the church are following these doctrines of demons.

2. (2-3) The nature of their departure from the faith and embrace of the doctrines of demons.

Speaking lies in hypocrisy, having their own conscience seared with a hot iron, forbidding to marry, *and commanding* to abstain from foods which God created to be received with thanksgiving by those who believe and know the truth.

a. **Speaking lies in hypocrisy**: This describes those who depart from the faith. This certainly points to the ones who willingly embrace falsehood to justify their sin or pride; but it also refers to those who *claim* to teach the Bible, while just using it to support their own ideas or agendas.

b. **Having their own conscience seared**: Their conscience, which at one time would have convicted them of their departure from the truth, now doesn't reply at all. It is as if the nerve endings of their conscience have been burnt over and are dead to feeling.

i. Paul here refers to the ancient practice of *branding* a criminal on the forehead with a distinguishing mark. For these, it was not their forehead that was branded with a hot iron, but their **conscience** instead.

ii. "They bear the marks of their hypocrisy as evidently and as indelibly in their conscience in the sight of God, as those who have been *cauterized* for their crimes do in their bodies in the sight of men." (Clarke)

iii. Paul knew what it was to have a dead, burned conscience. Before he surrendered his life to Jesus Christ on the road to Damascus, he felt completely justified in his persecution of Christians and hatred of Jesus. He could feel justified because his conscience was seared and needed a wake-up call – which the Lord graciously provided.

c. **Forbidding to marry, and commanding to abstain from foods**: This describes the *legalistic teaching* of those who have departed from the faith. They taught that it was by following this list of man-made rules that one was justified in God's sight – that you would be more holy to God if you didn't marry, and if you did not eat certain foods.

i. There have always been those in the church who regard themselves as more spiritual than God Himself, and have a stricter set of rules for living than God does.

ii. In the early centuries of the church, there were monks who went out to desolate desert places to show how spiritual they were by torturing themselves. One never ate cooked food. Another stood all night leaning on a sharp rock so that it was impossible for him to sleep. Another neglected his own body and allowed it to become so dirty that bugs dropped dead from his body. They did this because they thought it would win favor with God and show everyone how spiritual they were.

iii. We often think that if we sacrifice something for God (such as the right to marry or to eat certain foods), then He *owes* us something. This is legalism at its worst; trying to manipulate God into giving us something. The idea is that we can make God indebted to us, make Him our servant and make ourselves His master. In this we fulfill the original doctrine of demons – that we should be gods.

iv. Countless millions through the centuries have sought to sacrifice something, and make God owe them blessing, or forgiveness, or mercy, or whatever. That is the religion of self-flagellation; it is not the relationship with Jesus Christ described in the New Testament: *being justified freely by His grace through the redemption that is in Christ Jesus* (Romans 3:24).

v. "The controversy is not about flesh or fish, or about black or ashen colours, or about Wednesday or Friday, but about the mad superstitions of men who wish to obtain God's favour by such trifles and by contriving a carnal worship, invent for themselves an idol in God's place." (Calvin)

vi. **Forbidding to marry**: "They hold that it is far better for a priest to keep many whores than to have a wife." (Trapp)

3. (4-5) A refutation of the legalism that marks those who have departed from the faith.

For every creature of God *is* good, and nothing is to be refused if it is received with thanksgiving; for it is sanctified by the word of God and prayer.

a. **For every creature of God is good**: Regarding what we eat, we can eat all things. We receive things rightly when we receive them with **thanksgiving**, with an abiding sense of gratitude towards God. We receive the blessings of food, shelter, and comfort as gifts, and not as rights.

b. **Nothing is to be refused**: We are not limited by any kind of diet; what we eat does not make us more righteous before God (though what we eat may affect our health).

i. This issue was settled once for all when God spoke to Peter in Acts 10:9-16.

ii. "Both among the pagans, Jews, and Romanists, certain *meats* were prohibited; some *always*, others at *particular times*. This the apostle informs us was directly contrary to the original design of God; and says that those *who know the truth,* know this." (Clarke)

c. **It is sanctified by the word of God and prayer**: Paul here has in mind prayer before a meal. Notice that the emphasis is not on asking God to bless the food; but on thanking God for the blessing of providing food to eat.

i. The **word of God** sanctifies food in the sense that God gave two general commands to mankind to eat the good things of the earth.

- *And God said, "See, I have given you every herb that yields seed which is on the face of all the earth, and every tree whose fruit yields seed; to you it shall be for food."* (Genesis 1:29)

- *Every moving thing that lives shall be food for you. I have given you all things, even as the green herbs.* (Genesis 9:3)

ii. It is good and proper for us to pray before eating a meal but it should not be done in a ritualistic, superstitious way. Nor should it be done to show others how spiritual we are – which is imitating the prayer practices of the Pharisees (Matthew 6:5).

B. Instruction in ministry for Timothy.

1. (6) How to tell you are fulfilling your call.

If you instruct the brethren in these things, you will be a good minister of Jesus Christ, nourished in the words of faith and of the good doctrine which you have carefully followed.

a. **If you instruct the brethren in these things, you will be a good minister of Jesus Christ**: Notice that the pastor's job is primarily *instruction* of the *brethren*. If the minister does not **instruct the brethren in these things**, then he isn't really a **good minister of Jesus Christ**.

i. It is also important to say that *instruction* should be understood in a broad sense, not only as classroom-style teaching or Sunday preaching. Jesus instructed His disciples, but with His presence, His life, and His practice as well as with His words.

b. **Nourished in the words of faith and of the good doctrine which you have carefully followed**: But, if Timothy will be a **good minister of Jesus Christ**, he himself *must* remain anchored in God's word, carefully following **the good doctrine**.

2. (7-10) Keeping your priorities straight.

But reject profane and old wives' fables, and exercise yourself toward godliness. For bodily exercise profits a little, but godliness is profitable

for all things, having promise of the life that now is and of that which is to come. This *is* a faithful saying and worthy of all acceptance. For to this *end* we both labor and suffer reproach, because we trust in the living God, who is *the* Savior of all men, especially of those who believe.

a. **Reject profane and old wives' fables**: The priority must be on God's Word, not on the words of man. Paul cautioned Timothy to keep focused on the Word, not on things that come from man. The greatest effort must be put into God's Word, not man's word.

b. **Reject profane and old wives' fables**: This is the *negative* aspect of the command. In the *positive* aspect, the priority must be kept on eternal things, not temporal things.

c. **Exercise yourself toward godliness**: Ancient Greek and Roman culture put a high value on physical exercise. Paul tells Timothy that the same work and commitment that others put towards physical exercise should be put toward the pursuit of **godliness**.

i. "Here is an intentional paradox. Timothy is to meet the spurious asceticism of the heretics by *exercising himself in the practical piety of the Christian life*." (White)

ii. The word **godliness** comes from the old English word *Godlikeness*; it means to have the character and attitude of God. This was a worthy goal, much more worthy that the potential attainments of physical exercise.

iii. **Bodily exercise profits a little** in that it has *some* value. Or, the idea can be translated *bodily exercise is good for a while*, while exercising unto godliness is good for all eternity.

iv. Spiritual development and physical development share some similarities. With each, growth only comes with *exertion* and *proper feeding*.

d. **Godliness is profitable for all things, having promise of the life that now is**: Paul here explains the value of godliness, both in the present sense and its eternal sense. Godliness makes **the life that now is** better, and we should not hesitate to believe it and to tell people this.

i. Though godliness does not make this life the most comfortable, or richest, or most pleasurable, or easiest in **the life that now is**, it undeniably makes it the *best*, the *most contented*, and the most *fulfilling* life one can live in this world.

ii. "I assure you, and there are thousands of my brethren who can affirm the same, that after having tried the ways of sin, we infinitely prefer the ways of righteousness for their own pleasure's sake even here, and we would not change with ungodly men even if we had to die like dogs. With all the sorrow and care which Christian life is supposed to bring, we would prefer it to any other form of life beneath the stars." (Spurgeon)

e. **And of that which is to come**: At the same time, **godliness** is the *only guarantee* of a **profitable** life **which is to come**. There are many pleasures or achievements in this world that do not even pretend to offer anything for the life **which is to come**.

> i. Only godliness is the path to eternal life and happiness.

> - Sin and vice offer nothing for the life to come.
> - Genealogies and pedigrees offer nothing for the life to come.
> - Worldly success and wealth offer nothing for the life to come.
> - Personal fame or beauty offer nothing for the life to come.
> - Achievements in learning or the arts offer nothing for the life to come.

> ii. "Vice dares not say, it never has had the effrontery yet to say, 'Do evil and live in sin, and eternal life will come out of it.' No, the theater at its door does not proffer you eternal life, it invites you to the pit. The house of evil communications, the drunkard's bottle, the gathering-place of scorners, the chamber of the strange woman – none of these has yet dared to advertise a promise of eternal life as among the boons that may tempt its votaries. At best sin gives you but bubbles, and feeds you upon air. The pleasure vanishes, and the misery is left." (Spurgeon)

f. **We trust in the living God**: This is to be the great motto of the Christian life. Even as David challenged Goliath in the name of the living God (1 Samuel 17:26 and 36), so our **trust in the living God** empowers us to accomplish great things for His glory.

> i. "But *our* God, in whom we trust, is a God with a great, warm, loving heart, a thinking God, an active God, a working, personal God, who comes into the midst, of this world, and does not leave it to go on by itself. Although he is a stranger in the world, even as his people also are strangers and foreigners by reason of the revolt that men have made against their liege Lord and Sovereign, yet it is still his world, and he is still in it." (Spurgeon)

g. **The Savior of all men**: This emphasizes the idea that the priority must be kept on the message of Jesus Christ. It isn't that all men are saved in a

Universalist sense; but that there is only one **Savior** for all men. It isn't as if Christians have one Savior and others might have another savior.

i. But notice Paul's point: ***especially* of those who believe**. Jesus' work is *adequate* to save all, but only *effective* in saving those who come to Him by faith.

ii. "What God intends for ALL, he actually gives to *them* that believe in Christ, who died for the sins of the world [1 John 2:2], and tasted death for every man [Hebrews 2:9]. As *all* have been purchased by his blood so all may believe; and consequently all may be saved. Those that perish, perish through their own fault." (Clarke)

3. (11-16) Personal instructions.

These things command and teach. Let no one despise your youth, but be an example to the believers in word, in conduct, in love, in spirit, in faith, in purity. Till I come, give attention to reading, to exhortation, to doctrine. Do not neglect the gift that is in you, which was given to you by prophecy with the laying on of the hands of the eldership. Meditate on these things; give yourself entirely to them, that your progress may be evident to all. Take heed to yourself and to the doctrine. Continue in them, for in doing this you will save both yourself and those who hear you.

a. **These things command**: This has the note of authority. Timothy was not to enter the pulpit with speculations and opinions and theories of men. He was to fearlessly proclaim God's Word as a **command** and not give into the fear of man.

b. **Let no one despise your youth**: Because Timothy was young, he was vulnerable to the errors of youth which bring the often justified criticism of those older. To address this, Paul called him to live a life so that was so godly that no one could despise his youth.

i. The word **youth** in the ancient Greek was "Used of grown-up military age, extending to the 40th year" (Lock, cited in Earle). It seems that Timothy was about 30 years old at this time; but Paul was around 70, and youth is a relative thing.

ii. "St. Paul shows Timothy 'a more excellent way' than self-assertion for the keeping up of his dignity: Give no one any ground by any fault of character for despising thy youth." (White)

c. **Be an example to the believers**: The King James Version has *be thou an example of the believers*. Some believe this is a more accurate translation, with the idea being that Timothy was to be the best representation possible of the Christian community.

i. "The rendering of the King James, *an example of believers* is better." (Hiebert)

ii. This meant that Timothy, and every godly servant of God, should be an example:

- In what they say (**word**).
- In what they do (**conduct**).
- In their **love**.
- In their attitude (**spirit**).
- In their **faith** (in the sense of *faithfulness*).
- In their **purity**.

iii. *These* are the criteria by which to assess a pastor. If he is smart, if he is funny, if he is cool, if he dresses well, if he is popular, or if he is any number of other things matter little. You must look for a pastor who is an example in **word, in conduct, in love, in spirit, in faith, in purity**.

iv. "Thus we learn how foolish and ridiculous it is for people to complain that they receive no honour, when in fact there is nothing about them that is worth honouring, but rather they expose themselves to contempt by their ignorance, the example of their impure lives, their lightmindedness and other faults. The only way to win respect is by outstanding virtues which will protect us against contempt." (Calvin)

d. **Reading… exhortation… doctrine**: These are the things that Timothy must give attention to. Each of these things are centered on God's Word. He must **give attention** to these things in both his private life and in his public ministry.

e. **Do not neglect the gift that is in you**: Timothy was warned to not **neglect the gift** that God has given. This shows that there was definitely the *possibility* that gifts and abilities in him could be wasted for eternity. As with the parable of the talents, we should not bury what abilities God has given.

i. **Gift** is *charismatos* in the ancient Greek of the New Testament, and it refers to the varying spiritual gifts given to Timothy and to all believers. **Do not neglect the gift** has the idea that God gave Timothy supernatural gifts, and he should trust that God will do great things through him – learning to flow with the moving and leading of the Holy Spirit.

ii. "God's gifts groan under our disuse or misuse." (Trapp)

f. **With the laying on of hands**: Paul may have in mind Timothy's ordination service, when church leaders laid hands on him and recognized God's call on his life to ministry. This was an event apparently accompanied by prophecy.

i. "It is evident that the elders of the church at Lystra and Derbe had met together with the apostle Paul when Timothy was about to launch out into full-time service and had laid their hands on him, commending him to God in prayer." (Ironside)

g. **Meditate on these things**: Paul called Timothy to *meditation* on God's Word and the work of God in his life. This is not emptying our minds (the goal of Eastern meditation), but *filling* our minds with God's Word and truth.

h. **Give yourself entirely to them**: Timothy was encouraged to give it his all, to put forth a maximum effort, and by doing so, his **progress** would **be evident to all**. Often, progress is not evident because we do not give ourselves entirely to the pursuit of God and His will.

i. Often we fall short of all we can be for God because we are *passive* in our Christian life; we simply do not give ourselves entirely. Jesus warned against this passive attitude in the parable of the talents, where the servant who did nothing was severely rebuked.

ii. Paul could say, in 1 Corinthians 15:10: *But by the grace of God I am what I am, and His grace toward me was not in vain; but I labored more abundantly than they all, yet not I, but the grace of God which was with me.* Paul knew spiritual growth didn't just happen; it is the gift of God, but bestowed on those who actively pursue it.

iii. As Alan Redpath observed that a Christian might have a saved soul but a wasted life – but no follower of Jesus should ever be content with such a place.

iv. At the same time, we are careful to remember that giving our entire effort never *earns* the blessing or favor of God. Our hard work and heart work never puts God in the place where He owes us something. We give our entire effort out of gratitude and in honor to the God who has already done so much for us.

i. **Take heed**: Timothy, and every pastor, must examine constantly the two great areas of concern – one's **life** and one's **doctrine**. Failing to do this would mean danger for both Timothy himself and for those in his congregation.

i. Without giving heed to his **life**, Timothy might suffer shipwreck (as in 1 Timothy 1:19). Without giving heed to his **doctrine**, Timothy might lead others astray or leave them short of God's salvation.

ii. Those who **hear** Timothy as a pastor should be hearing **doctrine**. Timothy's primary call was not to entertain, amuse, or even help with practical things – it was to present Biblical doctrine, and to give heed to that doctrine.

j. **Save both yourself and those who hear you**: The benefit from taking heed to one's life and doctrine is remarkable. It is an assurance to the servant of God that they will also be saved, and many of **those who hear** them. Taken in the opposite, we see that the cost of failing to **take heed** to one's **life and doctrine** is high. The one who fails to **take heed** should feel no great assurance for either their own life or the lives of those who hear them.

i. "And just as the unfaithfulness or negligence of a pastor is fatal to the Church, so it is right for its salvation to be ascribed to his faithfulness and diligence. It is indeed true that it is God alone who saves and not even the smallest part of His glory can rightly be transferred to men. But God's glory is in no way diminished by His using the labour of men in bestowing salvation." (Calvin)

ii. "What a high honour is this to faithful ministers, that they should be styled saviours in a sense!" (Trapp)

iii. "For just as the salvation of his flock is a pastor's crown, so all that perish will be required at the hand of careless pastors." (Calvin)

iv. "Years ago Hamburgh was nearly half of it burned down, and among the incidents that happened, there was this one. A large house had connected with it a yard in which there was a great black dog, and this black dog in the middle of the night barked and howled most furiously. It was only by his barking that the family were awakened just in time to escape from the flames, and their lives were spared; but the poor dog was chained to his kennel, and though he barked and thus saved the lives of others, he was burned himself. Oh! Do not you who work for God in this church perish in that fashion. Do not permit your sins to enchain you, so that while you warn others you become lost yourselves." (Spurgeon)

1 Timothy 5 - How to Treat People in the Church

A. A summary of how to treat all people in the church.

1. (1) How to treat the men in the church.

Do not rebuke an older man, but exhort *him* as a father, younger men as brothers.

> a. **Do not rebuke and older man**: Paul directed Timothy that **older** men are generally not to be rebuked. A young pastor such as Timothy must shepherd them faithfully, but with due respect for the years and presumed wisdom of the **older** men.

>> i. Any godly person will show a deference to those who are aged. *You shall rise before the gray headed and honor the presence of an old man, and fear your God: I am the LORD* (Leviticus 19:32). *The silver-haired head is a crown of glory, if it is found in the way of righteousness* (Proverbs 16:31).

>> ii. There is another reason to exhort rather than rebuke an older man: he may simply not *receive* a rebuke.

> b. **Do not rebuke**: The ancient Greek verb for **rebuke** is not the normal word for "rebuke" in the New Testament. This is the only place this word is used, and it means literally "to strike at." Timothy was told to not attack older men with words, but to treat them with respect – as he would treat the younger men with respect as brothers.

>> i. The command was not that Timothy must never rebuke older men, but that he was not to strike at people with an overly harsh rebuke.

>> ii. Apart from this particularly severe word, in general *rebuke* is an important duty of a pastor. It is the simple, clear, presentation that someone is wrong, either in their conduct or thinking. Its main goal is not encouragement as much as to clearly confront someone with their wrong behavior or thinking. In another letter to a pastor, Paul made

the importance of rebuking clear: *Rebuke with all authority. Let no one despise you* (Titus 2:15).

iii. In 1 Timothy 5:20 – this very chapter – Timothy was told there are times are when not only an elder should be rebuked, but times when he should be rebuked publicly. Therefore, in this verse Timothy was not told to never rebuke, rather he was told to never rebuke in a harsh, attacking manner.

iv. The problem is that many people amass all their defensive ability at a rebuke – if not at the time, then later, after having time to think and listen to their pride. Some become experts at criticizing the one who brought the rebuke, and consider their hurt feelings more important than the truth of the rebuke.

v. No one likes to be rebuked; but the wise person uses the rebuke as a valuable means to growth. Spurgeon said, "A sensible friend who will unsparingly criticize you from week to week will be a far greater blessing to you than a thousand undiscriminating admirers if you have sense enough to bear his treatment, and grace enough to be thankful for it" (*Lectures to My Students*).

c. **But exhort him as a father**: Exhortation is encouragement to do what needs to be done. It has the manner of an encouraging coach or trainer, helping the athlete to achieve their best.

d. **Younger men**: These were to be treated as **brothers**; that is, as partners and friends in the work of the gospel, but without the same deference due to older men.

2. (2) How to treat women in the church.

Older women as mothers, younger as sisters, with all purity.

a. **Older women**: These were to be treated as **mothers**, with the respect and honor due their age. A young pastor must accept – and appreciate – some amount of mothering from some of the **older women** in the church, and it is proper to give them honor as such.

b. **The younger**: These younger women were to be treated **as sisters**; Timothy, as any godly man, was to always make certain his conduct towards younger women was always pure and above reproach. A godly man is not flirtatious or provocative and does not use double entendre' (witty words that can be taken in a flirtatious or provocative way).

B. How to treat widows and those in need.

1. (3) The general principle: help the needy who are truly in need.

Honor widows who are really widows.

a. **Honor widows**: In the days the New Testament was written, there was no social assistance system from the government. In that day there was one especially vulnerable class: elderly widows, who were usually without support from husbands or grown children, and without means to adequately support themselves. These are those **who are *really* widows**.

i. "One meaning of the word *to honour*, is *support, sustain*; and here it is most obviously to be taken in this sense." (Clarke)

ii. The principles revealed here are extremely relevant today, when many look to the local congregation as a place where the poor and needy should be able to come for financial help.

iii. Most any pastor can give you many stories about strangers who contact the church and ask for some kind of assistance – and pastors can tell you how hard it is to deal with such situations with love, but without being taken advantage of. The writer has had several experiences with the kind of men who call from a hotel with the big, sad story, pleading for money in the name of Christian love. Upon arrival, the room was usually a mess, the television turned to filth, and evidence of phone calls to churches called all around town, looking for pastors to tell the sad story. When asked to describe his favorite Bible verse, almost always the man would be confused and unable to answer. Upon many other occasions when helping those who are in need, the needy were asked to have their home church pastor call with a word of thanks – and it never happened.

b. **Who are really widows**: Those who were **really widows** were to receive **honor** – which in this context means financial support yet given in a dignified and honorable way.

2. (4-6) How to tell those who are really widows.

But if any widow has children or grandchildren, let them first learn to show piety at home and to repay their parents; for this is good and acceptable before God. Now she who is really a widow, and left alone, trusts in God and continues in supplications and prayers night and day. But she who lives in pleasure is dead while she lives.

a. **If any widow has children**: Those who should be legitimately helped by the church should not have family who can assist them. If they do have family to assist them, it is the responsibility of the family to do it.

i. This passage describes a "real" widow as one who is **left alone**; she has no one else to support her. "This shows that *widows indeed* are those that have *neither* children nor nephews, no relatives that either will or can help them, or no near relatives alive" (Clarke).

ii. **Let them first learn to show piety at home and to repay their parents** reminds us of the ongoing responsibility adult children have towards their parents and grandparents.

iii. "The Christian who falls below the best heathen standard of family affection is the more blameworthy, since he has, what the heathen has not, the supreme example of love in Jesus Christ." (White)

b. **Trusts in God and continues in supplications and prayers night and day**: Those who should be legitimately helped by the church should serve the church in some way. In this case, the widows would be given the job of praying for the church.

c. **But she who lives in pleasure**: Those who should be legitimately helped by the church must have godly lives. It is appropriate to say, "You're not living a godly life, so you won't receive financial assistance from the church."

i. "It does not indicate *grossly criminal pleasures*; but simply means one who indulges herself in *good eating and drinking*, pampering her body at the expense of her mind." (Clarke)

ii. **Is dead while she lives**: The life lived for mere pleasure and ease is no life at all. It is a living death, whether lived by a young widow or anyone else.

iii. Many who come to the church for assistance are in need because they have lived their lives for the pleasures of alcohol, drugs, or whatever; now they are in need and they want the church to help. It's legitimate to say, "No; you have lived **in pleasure** and now suffer the consequences. The resources of this congregation are not for your help in this case."

3. (7-8) Where provision should come from.

And these things command, that they may be blameless. But if anyone does not provide for his own, and especially for those of his household, he has denied the faith and is worse than an unbeliever.

a. **These things command**: A good pastor will teach these things, so all will know what God expects of them.

b. **If anyone does not provide for his own**: God's normal way of providing for the needy is not through the local congregation, but through our own hard work.

c. **He has denied the faith and is worse than an unbeliever**: In the strongest terms, Paul emphasized the responsibility of a man to provide for his family – to do all he could to support them.

i. This is the *minimum* required of a Christian man; if he does not do even this, his conduct is worse than an unbeliever's.

ii. "We may add that Jesus Himself gave an example of providing for one's own, when He provided a home for His mother with the beloved disciple." (White)

iii. This is why when someone is out of work, we can pray with such confidence, *knowing* it is God's will for them to provide for the needs of their family through work.

4. (9-10) Helping older widows.

Do not let a widow under sixty years old be taken into the number, *and not unless* she has been the wife of one man, well reported for good works: if she has brought up children, if she has lodged strangers, if she has washed the saints' feet, if she has relieved the afflicted, if she has diligently followed every good work.

a. **Do not let a widow under sixty years old be taken into the number**: The idea is that if someone is under sixty, they could still support themselves or get remarried. They did not need to be added to the support list of the church.

b. **Well reported for good works... if she has diligently followed every good work**: Those widows who were accepted into the support of the church must not only be true widows, but they must also have godly character. They were called to a job, not merely to a handout.

i. When Paul says that they she should have **brought up children**, he probably has in mind both the raising of one's own children, and the receiving of abandoned infants (which were all too common in the ancient world). "The words *brought up* may refer to the children of *others*, who were educated in the Christian faith by pious Christian women" (Clarke).

5. (11-16) Helping younger widows.

But refuse *the* younger widows; for when they have begun to grow wanton against Christ, they desire to marry, having condemnation because they have cast off their first faith. And besides they learn *to be* idle, wandering about from house to house, and not only idle but also gossips and busybodies, saying things which they ought not. Therefore I desire that *the* younger *widows* marry, bear children, manage the house, give no opportunity to the adversary to speak reproachfully. For some have already turned aside after Satan. If any believing man or woman has widows, let them relieve them, and do not let the church be burdened, that it may relieve those who are really widows.

a. **Refuse the younger widows**: As a general rule, these were not to be added to the support roll of the local congregation, because they generally could provide for themselves and could remarry.

i. Adam Clarke on the idea of "**grow wanton**": "The word is supposed to be derived from *to remove* and *the rein*; and is a metaphor taken from a pampered horse, from whose mouth the rein has been removed, so that there is nothing to check or confine him. The metaphor is plain enough, and the application easy."

b. **They desire to marry, having condemnation**: Paul did not condemn young widows for wanting to get married, only observing that many unmarried women are so hungry for marriage and companionship that they don't conduct themselves in a godly way in regard to relationships.

i. Many people get into a bad romance or spoil a friendship, because they are desperately needy for relationship. It's a common occurrence that Paul warned against.

ii. One doesn't have to be a young widow to fulfill the description of **they learn to be idle, wandering about from house to house, and not only idle but also gossips and busybodies, saying things which they ought not**. Those who spend much time talking about other people's lives need to get a life of their own. "It is no sin in any case to marry, bear children, and take care of a family; but it is a sin in every case to be idle persons, gadders about, tattlers, busybodies, sifting out and detailing family secrets" (Clarke).

iii. Paul did not condemn a young widow's desire for romantic companionship; but he insisted that it be pursued and expressed in the purity that should mark all believers.

c. **If any believing man or woman has widows, let them relieve them**: Paul concluded with a principle he alluded to three times in this section (1 Timothy 5:4, 5, and 8). The first responsibility for support is at the home; the local church is to support the truly destitute who are godly.

C. How to treat elders.

1. (17-18) Elders are to be honored according to principles from Scripture.

Let the elders who rule well be counted worthy of double honor, especially those who labor in the word and doctrine. For the Scripture says, "You shall not muzzle an ox while it treads out the grain," and, "The laborer *is* worthy of his wages."

a. **Elders**: The word here is to be understood in a broad sense of those in leadership. The focus is on elders **who rule** and elders who teach (**labor in**

the word and doctrine). Not necessarily will every elder who *rules* will also be an elder who *teaches*.

b. **Be counted worthy of double honor**: If an elder (such as a pastor) does **rule well** and does **labor in the word and doctrine** (clearly speaking of *hard work*), that one is worthy of **double honor**.

i. In this context, **double honor** means financial support. Paul already stated that certain widows were worthy of *honor* (1 Timothy 5:1), speaking of financial support. Now he added, **let the elders who rule well be counted worthy of double honor, especially those who labor in the word and doctrine**. Some think the church should not support pastors and staff, and that the paid ministry is an abomination – they say that the church instead should be using the money to support the needy. This is an attractive way of thinking; but it isn't Biblical. If the needy (that is, the *truly* needy) are worthy of honor, then those who properly rule and teach in the church are worthy of **double honor**.

ii. "Almost every critic of note allows that *timee* here signifies *reward, stipend, wages*. Let him have a double or a larger salary who rules well." (Clarke)

iii. White paraphrased Paul's idea: "What I have been saying about the support of widows reminds me of another question of Church finance: they payment of presbyters. Equity and scriptural principles suggest that they should be remunerated in proportion to their usefulness."

c. **For the Scripture says**: The principle that those who serve God's people should be paid (when possible, of course) is supported by the passages of **Scripture** quoted by Paul: Deuteronomy 25:4 and Luke 10:7.

i. Paul explained in 1 Corinthians 9:11 that if one sows spiritual things (such as **labor in the word and doctrine**), it is entirely appropriate for them to reap material things among those who they do the spiritual work. In Galatians 6:6 Paul wrote, *let him who is taught the word share in all good things with him who teaches*. In Philippians 4:17 Paul said that such giving abounds to the account of the giver, sharing in the reward of the spiritual ministry supported.

ii. It is also significant that Paul quoted Luke and called it **Scripture**, just as much as the passage from the Hebrew Scriptures that he referenced.

2. (19-20) How to treat a leader accused of sin.

Do not receive an accusation against an elder except from two or three witnesses. Those who are sinning rebuke in the presence of all, that the rest also may fear.

a. **Do not receive:** In these verses, Paul hit the balance between believing and acting on every bit of gossip that comes along about a leader in the church, and ignoring serious sin in a leader's life. Either extreme is wrong.

i. "Nothing does more harm than when some people are treated as if they could do no wrong and others as if they could do no right." (Barclay)

ii. "The reason of this difference is evident: those whose business it is to correct others will usually have many enemies; great caution, therefore, should be used in admitting accusations against such persons." (Clarke)

b. **Do not receive an accusation against an elder except from two or three witnesses**: Any accusation against a leader should not be automatically received. The accusation should be carefully verified by **two or three witnesses** – not just two or three others who also heard the gossip. Timothy should not **receive** or promote unsubstantiated accusations about church leaders.

i. In his commentary on 1 Timothy, John Calvin explained some reasons why people are so quick to **receive an accusation** against a pastor when perhaps they should not: "The more sincerely any pastor strives to further Christ's kingdom, the more he is loaded with spite, the more fierce do the attacks upon him become. And not only so, but as soon as any charge is made against ministers of the Word, it is believed as surely and firmly as if it had been already proved. This happens not only because a higher standard of integrity is required from them, but because Satan makes most people, in fact nearly everyone, over credulous so that without investigation, they eagerly condemn their pastors whose good name they ought to be defending."

ii. Calvin pointed out there is a spiritual attack in all of this: "It is indeed a trick of Satan to estrange men from their ministers so as gradually to bring their teaching into contempt. In this way not only is wrong done to innocent people whose reputation is undeservedly injured, but the authority of God's holy teaching is diminished."

iii. There is an old story about a pastor who was trying to defend himself against criticism. He said, "There's a story going about that I told my wife not to go to a certain church that has wild meetings. They say my wife went anyway, and I dragged her out of the church by her hair, and I hurt her so badly she had to go to the hospital. Let me respond to these accusations. First of all, I never told her to stay away from that church. Second, I didn't drag her out by her hair. Third, she never had to go to the hospital. Lastly, I've never been married so I don't have a wife."

iv. Spurgeon advised in *Lectures to My Students* that when people come to a pastor with gossip, he should say, "Well, all this is very important, and I need to give it my full attention – but my memory isn't so good and I have a lot to think about. Can you write it all down for me?" Spurgeon says this will take care of it, because they won't want to write down their gossip.

c. **Those who are sinning rebuke in the presence of all, that the rest may fear**: However, if leaders are in sin, it must be addressed forthrightly - with public rebuke, to promote a fear of sin among the leadership and the entire church.

i. Many congregations have had great trouble because sin in the leadership was not forthrightly dealt with. It's important that everyone understand that leadership in the church does not shield one from accountability; it makes one even more accountable.

ii. According to John Calvin, in the Middle Ages the church protected its corrupt bishops against accusation by demanding that 72 witnesses be brought forth to confirm any accusation against a bishop. This is an extreme example of corrupt leaders protecting other corrupt leaders.

3. (21) Do not be prejudiced or show partiality.

I charge *you* before God and the Lord Jesus Christ and the elect angels that you observe these things without prejudice, doing nothing with partiality.

a. **I charge you before God and the Lord Jesus Christ and the elect angels**: This strong statement reflects the serious nature of the job of leaders in the local congregation. They serve an eternal God and must please Him first in everything they do.

i. "We are safe in saying that *the elect angels* are identical with 'the angels which kept their own principality' (Jude 6), 'that did not sin' (2 Pet. 2:4)." (White)

ii. "He adds to Christ the angels, not that they are judges, but as future witnesses of carelessness or rashness or self-seeking or bad faith. They are present as spectators, for they have been given charge to care for the Church." (Calvin)

iii. "And indeed the man who is not shaken out of his carelessness and laziness by the thought that the government of the Church is conducted under the eye of God and His angels must be worse than stupid, and have his heart harder than stone." (Calvin)

b. **Observe these things without prejudice, doing nothing with partiality**: **Prejudice** and **partiality** are grave sins before God. In the New Testament, the emphasis is on **partiality** according to class (James 2:1-9); but partiality according to race and gender is also included (Galatians 3:26-29) and regarded as sin.

i. "Do not treat any man, in religious matters, according to the rank he holds in life, or according to any personal attachment thou mayest have for him. Every man should be dealt with in the church as he will be dealt with at the judgment-seat of Christ." (Clarke)

D. How to treat potential leaders in the church.

1. (22) Be careful about approving the ministry of another person.

Do not lay hands on anyone hastily, nor share in other people's sins; keep yourself pure.

a. **Lay hands on anyone**: This is used in the sense of ordination. Paul cautioned Timothy to let a man prove himself before he was recognized in ministry. There should not be a rush; time must season a man and his ministry.

i. Some think the admonition **do not lay hands on anyone hastily** has to do with receiving repentant people back into the fellowship of the church. It seems that in some early church circles, those who had fallen into scandalous sin had to be received back into the church with the laying on of hands and prayer by church leaders. If so, Paul meant, "Don't go too fast. Let them demonstrate their repentance first."

b. **Lay hands on**: Since ordination simply recognizes God's calling, it is all the more reason to not be in a hurry – time should be given to allow those gifts and callings to demonstrate themselves.

i. It isn't uncommon for a young man in the ministry to be a bit impatient; he wants to do great things for the Lord and is anxious for pastors and elders to **lay hands** on them in recognition of God's work in them.

ii. Yet, there is danger if anyone *waits* to give themselves fully to serving the Lord until they are recognized with a title or the laying on of hands. This means they are more concerned with *image* (how it appears to others) than with *substance* (what they can really be doing for the Lord right now).

c. **Keep yourself pure**: This connects to an important idea. If Timothy was called to observe and assess the lives of others, it was important that he pay even more attention to his own life.

i. "The intention of the warning would be that Timothy would best avoid clerical scandals by being cautious at the outset as to the character of those whom he ordains." (White)

ii. **Nor share in other people's sins**: We all have enough sin of our own; we do not need to add to it by partaking in the sins of others. There are many ways we can do this.

- We can share in the sins of others by setting a bad example before them.
- We can share in the sins of others by approving of them or ignoring them.
- We can share in the sins of others by joining a church that spreads dangerous teachings.

2. (23) Paul's medical advice to Timothy.

No longer drink only water, but use a little wine for your stomach's sake and your frequent infirmities.

a. **Use a little wine for your stomach's sake**: Water in the ancient world was often impure and Timothy probably had problems from the impure water. Since the fermentation process would eliminate some of the harmful things in the water, it would be better for him to drink **a little wine** rather than water all the time.

b. **Use a little wine**: Timothy was probably abstaining from alcohol for the sake of setting a good example. However, this abstinence was hurting his health – wine was safer to drink than water. So, Paul told Timothy that it wasn't wise to sacrifice his health for the sake of this abstinence – he would do more good for the Jesus and His kingdom by taking care of his body in this circumstance.

i. "Paul is simply saying that there is no good in an asceticism which does the body more harm than good." (Barclay)

c. **Your frequent infirmities**: Timothy was the victim of **frequent infirmities**; yet Paul did not simply command a healing on apostolic authority, or even send him a handkerchief with healing power (Acts 19:11-12). This demonstrates that Paul did not have miraculous powers at his own command, but only at the prompting of the Holy Spirit. Apparently, there was no such prompting in Timothy's case.

i. If it is God's will for all to be healed *right now*, then Paul (and the Holy Spirit who inspired him) here led Timothy into sin – calling him to look to a natural remedy instead of a divine healing. God uses natural remedies and the work of doctors in healing, as well as the supernatural power of the Holy Spirit – they don't contradict one another.

3. (24-25) The difficulty in looking at a man's sin and his good works.

Some men's sins are clearly evident, preceding *them* to judgment, but those of some *men* follow later. Likewise, the good works *of some* are clearly evident, and those that are otherwise cannot be hidden.

a. **Some men's sins are clearly evident... but those of some men follow later**: It is easy to see the struggles and sins some have; but with some others, the sins are hidden.

i. We all have areas of our lives God is dealing with; and sometimes the area is something clearly evident to others. But sometimes the sinful area is not evident; some people are regarded as holy just because they are good at hiding their sin.

b. **Otherwise cannot be hidden**: Good works are always eventually revealed; but sins are sometimes hidden and will be evident only at the judgment. These words are meant to be a caution to Timothy in his appointing of leaders. Sometimes what one sees on the outside isn't really an accurate picture, so we need to take it slow, so we can wait on God for discernment.

1 Timothy 6 - Riches and Godliness

A. A word to servants.

1. (1) A word to slaves in general.

Let as many bondservants as are under the yoke count their own masters worthy of all honor, so that the name of God and *His* doctrine may not be blasphemed.

> a. **Let as many bondservants**: Paul called upon slaves to **count their own masters worthy of all honor** - to be good, respectful workers for their masters. He did this not out of a general approval of the institution of slavery, but so that God would be glorified (**so that the name of God and His doctrine may not be blasphemed**).

> > i. Christianity arose in a social setting where slavery was commonplace. There were some 60 million slaves in the Roman Empire. Some slaves held privileged positions; other slaves were treated with great abuse. While the Bible never commanded slavery, it did permit it and regulate it.

> > ii. Jesus, Paul and others in the New Testament did not call for a violent revolution against the institution of slavery (which perhaps, humanly speaking, might have failed miserably). Yet through the transformation brought by the gospel, they did effectively destroy the foundations of slavery – racism, greed, class hatred – and made a civilization without slavery possible.

> > iii. The church itself was a place where slavery was destroyed. It was not uncommon for a master and a slave to go to church together, where the slave would be an elder in the church, and the master was expected to submit to the slave's spiritual leadership! Such radical thinking was an offense to many, but glorified God and eventually destroyed slavery.

b. **As are under the yoke**: These same principles apply to our occupations today. When we work hard and honor our employers, it glorifies God. But when we are bad workers and disrespectful to our supervisors, it brings shame on the name of Jesus Christ.

> i. Colossians 3:22-24 gives the sense of this: *Servants, obey in all things your masters according to the flesh, not with eye-service, as men-pleasers, but in sincerity of heart, fearing God. And whatever you do, do it heartily, as to the Lord and not to men, knowing that from the Lord you will receive the reward of the inheritance; for you serve the Lord Christ.* No matter who we work for, we really work for the Lord - and we should give the Lord both honor and a hard day of work.

c. **So that the name of God and His doctrine may not be blasphemed**: People will judge Christianity – who God is (**the name of God**) and what the Bible teaches (**and His doctrine**) – based on how believers conduct themselves as workers.

> i. Each Christian should ask if they are leading people *to* Jesus by how they work, or if they are leading people *away* from Jesus by their bad work and testimony at their job.

2. (2) A special word to slaves with Christian masters.

And those who have believing masters, let them not despise *them* because they are brethren, but rather serve *them* because those who are benefited are believers and beloved. Teach and exhort these things.

a. **And those who have believing masters**: Perhaps it was easy for a slave to say, "My master doesn't know Jesus. That's why he expects me to work so hard." But if the master were a Christian, or became a Christian, the slave might think, "My brother shouldn't expect me to work so hard now; he will show me Christian love, and perhaps favor me above the other slaves, because I am a Christian also."

b. **Let them not despise them because they are brethren, but rather serve them**: We can almost imagine a slave saying, "My master is my brother! We are equal before the Lord. He has no right to tell me what to do." This attitude ignores the fact that God calls us into many relationships where submission is commanded - in the home, in the church, in the workplace. Our equality in Jesus doesn't eliminate God's order of authority.

c. **But rather serve them because those who are benefited are believers and beloved**: Upon this principle, Christian slaves with Christian masters were not free to despise their masters for expecting them to work, and to work hard. Rather, the slave should be even more dedicated to work because he served a brother.

i. We should never expect special treatment because our boss or supervisor is a Christian. Instead, that should motivate us to work all the harder, because we can then be a blessing to another brother.

ii. Warren Wiersbe relates the story of a young lady who had left a secular job to work for a Christian organization. She had been there about a month and was really disillusioned. "I thought it was going to be heaven on earth," she complained. "Instead, there are nothing but problems." Wiersbe asked her if she was working just as hard for her new boss as she did in the secular job. The look on her face said, "No!" So, Wiersbe told her, "Try working harder, and show your boss real respect. Just because all of you in the office are saved doesn't mean you can do less than your best." She took his advice and the problems cleared up.

d. **Teach and exhort these things**: This teaching was especially important in the ancient world, where slaves might be treated very differently from master to master, and where there was sometimes intense racism and hatred between slaves and masters.

B. Money, contentment and godliness.

1. (3-5) Warning against those who misuse God's word.

If anyone teaches otherwise and does not consent to wholesome words, *even* the words of our Lord Jesus Christ, and to the doctrine which accords with godliness, he is proud, knowing nothing, but is obsessed with disputes and arguments over words, from which come envy, strife, reviling, evil suspicions, useless wranglings of men of corrupt minds and destitute of the truth, who suppose that godliness is a *means of* gain. From such withdraw yourself.

a. **If anyone teaches otherwise**: In drawing to the close of the letter, Paul referred again to a theme he mentioned in the first chapter – that Timothy must be on guard against those who would misuse the word of God.

i. **Teaches otherwise** in this context may mean replacing the plain teaching of God's word with a focus on prophecies and visions and strange spiritual experiences people claim. This was a great danger that Paul warned Timothy against.

ii. Poole on **if anyone teaches otherwise**: "If there be any person who either more publicly or more privately shall take upon him to instruct people otherwise." Some of the most dangerous teaching in the church isn't done from a pulpit, but in informal, private conversations.

b. **And does not consent to wholesome words**: Paul warned Timothy against the argumentative heretic, who has left the word of God to promote his own ideas – who **does not consent to wholesome words, even the words of our Lord Jesus Christ**. He warned Timothy against those who seemed to treat the Word of God more as a plaything instead of as a precious gift.

i. You don't have to be an active opponent of God's word to be an enemy of it. If we fail to give the Bible its rightful place in our life and in our preaching, we oppose God's word.

ii. "It is possible not to profess any ungodly or manifest error and yet to corrupt the doctrine of godliness by silly boastful babbling. For when there is no progress or edification from any teaching, it has already departed from the institution of Christ." (Calvin)

c. **Even the words of our Lord Jesus Christ**: This might seem like an unnecessary warning against an obvious danger. Yet the warning was necessary, because those who misuse God's truth don't advertise themselves that way. They often claim to honor God's word while in fact misusing it.

i. There are different ways that people do **not consent** to the truth of God's Word.

- Some *deny* God's Word.
- Some *ignore* God's Word.
- Some *explain away* God's Word.
- Some *twist* God's Word using it as a toy to be played with in debate and disputes.

ii. One can be surrounded by God's truth; one can even memorize the Bible, and *not* have it effect the life for eternity. Curiosity or interest in God's Word without submission to it is a grave danger.

iii. In our day – a time when we are overwhelmed with useless information – it is easy to regard the Bible as useless information or as a source of answers to trivia questions, but not as a book with truth that confronts and transforms my life. Bible study is *not* trivial pursuit; to treat the Bible as a book of useless information is to misuse it.

d. **He is proud, knowing nothing**: This describes those who misuse God's Word. Yet, as all the proud, they don't see or admit to their lack of knowledge. And, like most proud people, they are able to convince others that they are *experts* in God's truth, when they actually misuse it.

i. To not allow God's Word to speak for itself – to put your own "spin" on it as modern politicians and public relations people do – is the worst kind of pride. It shows someone has more confidence in their own wisdom and opinions than in the straightforward truth of God. Surely, these proud people are those **knowing nothing**.

ii. It is nothing but *pride* that could make the preacher think that their stories, their anecdotes, their opinions, or their humor could be more important than the clear Word of God. Such stories and anecdotes and humor must be used to present the clear Word of God, not to replace it.

e. **Obsessed with disputes and arguments**: Those who misuse God's Word may be expert debaters on their current doctrinal hobby-horse; but their desire to constantly debate some aspect of doctrine shows their unwillingness to humbly receive the truth.

i. Paul isn't speaking about people who inquire or question in a genuine desire to learn; but those who ask questions or start discussion mainly to show others how smart they are.

f. **Envy, strife, reviling, evil suspicions**: This is the fruit of the **disputes and arguments** of those who misuse God's truth. Their presence in a church body is the source of all kinds of division and discontent; though they may appear to be experts on the Bible, they actually do damage to God's church. Therefore, Paul warned Timothy, "**From such withdraw yourself**."

i. Timothy should expect that such men would:

- **Envy** him and his office (without admitting to it).
- That they would create **strife** among the Christians.
- That they would promote **reviling** of Timothy and other leaders in the church.
- That they would be the source of **evil suspicions** - always suspecting Timothy and other leaders in the church of evil motives and plots.

ii. Timothy needed this warning, because such dangerous people are not as obvious as one might think.

iii. **Useless wranglings**: "Endless and needless discourses... The Greek word signifieth galling one another with disputes, or rubbing one against another, as scabbed sheep will, and so spreading the infection" (Trapp).

g. **Who suppose that godliness is a means of gain**: This is another characteristic of those who misuse God's truth. Their interest in the things of God is not entirely for God's glory but motivated in part by desire for wealth and comfort.

i. "For these men all Christianity is to be measured by the gains it brings… Paul forbids the servants of Christ to have any dealings with such men." (Calvin)

ii. Christianity is commonly presented today on the basis of what you will *gain* by following Jesus: personal success and happiness, a stronger family, a more secure life. These things may be true to some degree, but we must never market the gospel as a product that will fix every life problem.

iii. When the gospel is marketed this way, it makes followers of Jesus who are completely unprepared for tough times. After all, if the "Jesus product" isn't working, why not try another brand? Also, this sales approach takes the focus off Jesus Himself, and puts the focus on what He will give us. Many have their hearts set on the blessings, not the One who blesses us.

iv. While not ignoring the blessings of following Jesus Christ, we must proclaim the need to follow Jesus because He is God, and we owe Him everything as our Creator. What is right before God, and what glorifies Him, is more important than whatever benefit we may gain.

v. We need to see Christians who are more concerned with what glorifies God than with what benefits me.

h. **From such withdraw yourself**: Timothy is told to deliberately *not* associate with those who receive or present the gospel with this kind of marketing approach.

i. "He does not only forbid Timothy from imitating them, but tells him to avoid them as harmful pests. Although they do not openly oppose the Gospel, but make a profession of it, yet their company is infectious. Besides, if the crowd sees us to be familiar with these men, there is a danger that they will use our friendship to insinuate themselves into its favour. We should therefore take great pains to make everyone understand that we are quite different from them, and have nothing at all in common with them." (Calvin)

2. (6) The true gain of godliness.

Now godliness with contentment is great gain.

a. **Now godliness**: Paul told Timothy that those who misuse God's Word wrongly think godliness is a means of material gain. Knowing his statement might be misunderstood, he followed up with an explanation.

b. **Now godliness with contentment is great gain**: It is true that godliness is **great gain**; but only when accompanied by **contentment**.

i. "The word here used for *contentment* is *autarkeia*… By it they meant a complete *self-sufficiency*. They meant a frame of mind which was completely independent of all outward things, and which carried the secret of happiness within itself. Contentment never comes from the possession of external things." (Barclay)

c. **With contentment**: When one does not live by "the itch for more," and one's life is not dominated by shopping for and acquiring material things, we can have the kind of **contentment** in God and in His will for our lives.

i. This is a slippery area in the Christian life. It is very easy to come up with reasons – excuses, that is – why these sins of greed and materialism don't apply to us. But whenever we think getting something material, or getting more of it, will answer our life's needs, we lack this contentment. Whenever we are deeply grieved at material loss, we lack this contentment. Whenever we get an inordinate pleasure from buying or having some material thing, we lack this contentment.

d. **Godliness with contentment is great gain**: Paul knew this kind of **contentment** first hand; here is his testimony in Philippians 4:11-13: *Not that I speak in regard to need, for I have learned in whatever state I am, to be content: I know how to be abased, and I know how to abound. Everywhere and in all things I have learned both to be full and to be hungry, both to abound and to suffer need. I can do all things through Christ who strengthens me.*

i. It is true that material possessions in and of themselves do not corrupt us; Paul could *abound* in material things and still keep it all in proper perspective. But too many use this truth to excuse their own materialism and carnal lack of contentment.

ii. **Contentment** is essential, and difficult for many reasons:

- We can only find contentment when our hearts are rooted in eternal things; and contentment is essential because it shows we are living with an eternal perspective, not only trying to feather an earthly nest.

- It is hard to be content, because our consumer culture feeds our lack of contentment, by rewarding us when we are discontent, and with advertising that tries to make us feel discontent without a product.

- It is hard to be content, because we almost always desire far more than we need.

e. **Godliness with contentment is great gain**: Godliness really can bring almost unbelievable contentment; but before it can, we must be *transformed* *by the renewing of your mind* (Romans 12:2) – to start putting material things in their proper priority next to spiritual things.

i. It's easy for many Christians to say they have this contentment; but whether they have it or not is often more truthfully known by their spending and shopping habits. How much of a place does shopping and buying have in your life? How does material loss affect your happiness? How happy do you get from having some material thing?

ii. When we live and act without contentment, we are trying to fill needs in our lives – a need to be "somebody," a need to feel secure or cared for, a need to have excitement and newness in our lives – most people try to fulfill these needs with material things, but they can only really be met by a spiritual relationship with the God who made us.

iii. Real **contentment** isn't too difficult for those whose real home is heaven. "It requires but little of this world's goods to satisfy a man who feels himself to be a citizen of another country, and knows that this is not his *rest*" (Clarke).

3. (7-8) The heart of contentment.

For we brought nothing into *this* world, *and it is* certain we can carry nothing out. And having food and clothing, with these we shall be content.

a. **We brought nothing into this world**: A baby is born not only penniless, but without even a pocket to put pennies in. Just as certainly, **we can carry nothing out** – the things that make a man rich in this world mean nothing in the world to come.

b. **It is certain we can carry nothing out**: A heart of contentment begins with seeing our material possessions and resources in an *eternal* perspective.

i. It has been wisely observed that a moving trailer never follows a hearse. Everything one might take with them to the world beyond is left behind. Gold is a precious commodity on earth; in heaven God uses it to pave the streets.

ii. Jesus once told a parable that has troubled some people. In Luke 16:1-14, He spoke of a dishonest manager, who was about to be called to account. Knowing he will be fired, he began to settle accounts with his master's debtors at terms favorable to the debtors, so they would treat him kindly when the master fired him. The master ended up complimenting the manager for his shrewd tactics (presumably before he fired him). The manager was praiseworthy for two reasons. First, he knew he would be called to account for his life and he took it seriously. Secondly, he took advantage of his *present* position to arrange a comfortable *future*. We can use our material resources *right now* for eternal good – even though we can't bring them with us.

iii. We **can carry nothing out** – but we can *send ahead* eternal blessing and reward through wise use of our resources right now.

c. **Having food and clothing**: After an eternal perspective, a heart of contentment will be humble, a heart that can be content with simple things.

i. Most of us become jaded over the years, and our over-stimulated culture is effective at producing this in us. Things that used to satisfy us are no longer good enough. The constant hunger for more and more, for more and better, for new and improved, all work against real contentment.

4. (9-10) The folly of the greedy heart.

But those who desire to be rich fall into temptation and a snare, and *into* many foolish and harmful lusts which drown men in destruction and perdition. For the love of money is a root of all *kinds of* evil, for which some have strayed from the faith in their greediness, and pierced themselves through with many sorrows.

a. **Those who desire to be rich**: Significantly, the **desire** for riches is far more dangerous than the riches themselves – and it isn't only the poor who desire to be rich, it is also the rich who want *more* riches.

i. Poor does not mean godly and rich ungodly; nor is it true the other way around. There were many remarkably godly men in the Bible who were almost unbelievably rich, such as Abraham, David, and Solomon.

ii. But the godly rich have the heart like the Psalmist in Psalm 62:10: *If riches increase, do not set your heart on them.*

b. **Those who desire to be rich fall into temptation and a snare**: This desire for riches tempts our heart away from eternal riches and ensnares us in a trap few can escape – always dreaming of riches, and always setting one's heart on them.

i. The **desire to be rich** can really only be satisfied in Jesus Christ and satisfied with spiritual riches rather than material ones. Everything else falls short.

c. **The love of money is a root of all kinds of evil**: The love of money can motivate any evil on this earth. There is no sin that cannot be committed for the sake of money.

d. **Pierced themselves through with many sorrows**: This is the fate of those who live in the love of money. They are *not* satisfied. We sometimes want the opportunity to find out if riches can satisfy, but we should trust the Word of God and the experience of many.

> i. "So do these strangle, drown, poison their precious souls with profits, pleasures, and preferments, and many times meet with perdition and destruction, that is, with a double destruction, temporal and eternal, as some expound it." (Trapp)

5. (11-16) True riches: serving a Great King.

But you, O man of God, flee these things and pursue righteousness, godliness, faith, love, patience, gentleness. Fight the good fight of faith, lay hold on eternal life, to which you were also called and have confessed the good confession in the presence of many witnesses. I urge you in the sight of God who gives life to all things, and *before* Christ Jesus who witnessed the good confession before Pontius Pilate, that you keep *this* commandment without spot, blameless until our Lord Jesus Christ's appearing, which He will manifest in His own time, *He who is* the blessed and only Potentate, the King of kings and Lord of lords, who alone has immortality, dwelling in unapproachable light, whom no man has seen or can see, to whom *be* honor and everlasting power. Amen.

a. **But you, O man of God**: Timothy was commanded to be different from those who lived for riches and material wealth. He was to **flee** the proud arguments of those who misuse God's Word and who suppose that we should follow God just for what we can get out of it.

b. **Pursue righteousness, godliness, faith, love, patience, gentleness**: Instead of pride and riches, Timothy was to make these things his pursuit. These are things which are often not valued in our present age but are very valuable to God.

> i. This challenge to leave some things and follow hard after some other things isn't just directed to Timothy, but to everyone who would be a **man** [or woman] **of God** – as opposed to being a man of *this* world.

c. **Fight the good fight of faith**: Going God's way – against the flow of this world – won't be easy. Therefore, Timothy had to have a soldier's determination.

> i. God calls us to be fighters, but to fight **the good fight of faith** – a fight where some may lose a battle here and there, but they will carry on the fight with great determination until the war is over – when we **lay hold on eternal life**.

> ii. Timothy was drafted into this war: **To which you were also called**. But Timothy also volunteered: **And have confessed the good confession in the presence of many witnesses**. Timothy had to

consider both so as to set his thinking right for the fight. God had called him, and he had also freely chosen.

d. **In the sight of God who gives life to all things**: Since Paul called Timothy to a difficult battle, it was good for him to know that the orders were given under this great God. Timothy had an obligation to serve the Creator who gave him life.

i. The denial of God as Creator has done wide damage in our culture. Some of the biggest damage has come from the simple fact that many people no longer believe they have a Creator they must honor and be accountable to.

e. **Christ Jesus**: This was *who gave* Timothy the difficult command. Jesus Himself knew what it was to fulfill a difficult command, because He **witnessed the good confession before Pontius Pilate** and Jesus did it in several ways.

i. Jesus admitted the truth about Himself, agreeing with Pilate's statement that Jesus was the King of the Jews (Matthew 27:11).

ii. Jesus testified to Pilate about the sovereignty of God, saying *You could have no power at all against Me unless it had been given to you from above* (John 19:11). Jesus let Pilate know that God was in charge, not Pilate.

iii. Jesus was silent about specific accusations, refusing to defend Himself, but leaving His life in the will of God the Father (Matthew 27:14). "For Christ made His *confession before Pilate* not in many words but in reality, that is by His voluntary submission to death" (Calvin).

iv. In each of these ways, Jesus made a *good confession before Pontius Pilate*. When Timothy was told to live up to the *good confession* he made (1 Timothy 6:12), he was simply told to do what Jesus did.

f. **Until our Lord Jesus Christ's appearing**: This was *how long* Timothy was supposed to fight the good fight. There is always danger that a good effort will simply not last long enough, and end in defeat.

g. **He who is**: Knowing who Jesus is equipped Timothy to fight the good fight. History is filled with example of armies that have been led to spectacular victories because the men knew and loved their leaders. Therefore, here Paul described Jesus to Timothy.

i. He is **the blessed and only Potentate** – the One who alone has all power and strength, who rules over the universe from an occupied throne in heaven.

ii. He is the **King of kings and Lord of lords**; the majesty of man fades in comparison to the glory of Jesus. The richest, smartest, most influential persons on earth are midgets next to King Jesus.

iii. He **alone has immortality, dwelling in unapproachable light, whom no man has seen or can see**: He is holy. Jesus is not merely a super-man, He is the God-man; truly immortal without beginning or end; with a glory which if fully revealed would strike any human dead.

iv. **To whom be honor and everlasting power**: Knowing who this Jesus is should bring forth a response - not primarily, "what can He do for me?" but a response of simple and profound *worship* – declaring **honor and everlasting power** towards this great God. **Amen!**

h. **To whom be honor and everlasting power**: Paul praised the glory and honor of the exalted, enthroned Lord Jesus Christ. He is a unique man (**who alone has immortality**) and a glorified man (**unapproachable light**).

6. (17-19) A final word to the rich.

Command those who are rich in this present age not to be haughty, nor to trust in uncertain riches but in the living God, who gives us richly all things to enjoy. *Let them* do good, that they be rich in good works, ready to give, willing to share, storing up for themselves a good foundation for the time to come, that they may lay hold on eternal life.

a. **Rich in this present age**: This phrase puts it all in perspective. These ones might be rich now, but they must use their riches responsibly if they will be rich in the age to come.

b. **Not to be haughty**: Pride is a constant danger with riches. It is very easy to believe that we *are* more because we *have* more than another man has.

c. **Nor to trust in uncertain riches but in the living God**: God knows our tendency to trust in riches instead of in Him. He guards us against this danger because He wants us to trust in that which is most certain – in Him and not in **uncertain riches**.

d. **Let them do good, that they be rich in good works, ready to give**: Being a giver, and doing good with our resources is what guards our heart from materialism and trusting in uncertain riches.

i. Many think the main reason for giving unto the Lord is because the church needs money. That isn't true. The most important reason to give is because *you* need to be a giver. It is God's way of guarding you against greed and trust in uncertain riches. God will provide for His work even if you do not give; but what will happen to *you*?

ii. If you do not give of your material things to the Lord's work, how will you be **storing up for** [yourself] **a good foundation for the time to come**? How will you **lay hold on eternal life**? Will there not be some – perhaps many – who do not enter heaven because they heart was really far more comfortable here on earth with its material rewards?

e. **Lay hold on eternal life**: Paul's idea was to Timothy, "Leave the pursuit of money aside and be content with your work as a minister of the gospel. Your hand is not big enough to lay hold of two things. Therefore, since you can only have one, see that it is the vital thing. Lay hold on eternal life."

i. "From this it is evident that if he lays hold on eternal life, he will have to fight for it; and that if he has to fight, he can only fight by laying hold upon eternal life with tenacious grip." (Spurgeon)

7. (20-21) Conclusion: A final charge.

O Timothy! Guard what was committed to your trust, avoiding the profane *and* idle babblings and contradictions of what is falsely called knowledge—by professing it some have strayed concerning the faith. Grace *be* with you. Amen.

a. **O Timothy!** Paul repeated a theme often used, challenging Timothy to distinguish between what comes from God (**that which was committed to your trust**), and what comes from man (**vain babblings**); and to guard against becoming enamored with what comes from man.

i. Paul had confidence in Timothy and he did trust him. Yet Paul also knew how great the power of seduction is, and how high the stakes are - so he warned, and warned, and warned again.

b. **Guard what was committed to your trust**: The gospel is a **trust** committed to pastors like Timothy; but also, to all believers. And when that trust is broken, **some have strayed concerning the faith**. We must do all that we can to keep this **trust**.

2 Timothy 1 – A Spirit of Boldness

A. Greeting and introduction.

1. (1) A letter from Paul.

Paul, an apostle of Jesus Christ by the will of God, according to the promise of life which is in Christ Jesus.

a. **Paul, an apostle of Jesus Christ by the will of God**: Paul's introduction here is like his other letters, with an immediate declaration that he is an **apostle** according to **the will of God**, not according to his own ambition or man's choice.

i. Paul had a role to play in God's plan for reaching the world for Jesus Christ, and his role was **apostle** – being a unique ambassador from God to the world. Everyone has their own role to play, and we much each fulfill it **by the will of God**.

b. **According to the promise of life**: This statement is unique compared to greetings in Paul's other letters. It was appropriate here because Paul was imprisoned again in Rome and he expected to be executed (2 Timothy 4:6). Therefore, this **promise of life** was especially precious to him.

i. The Bible doesn't tell us the details, but it seems that after Paul was released from the Roman imprisonment mentioned at the end of the book of Acts, he enjoyed a few more years of liberty until he was re-arrested and imprisoned in Rome again.

ii. One can go to Rome today and see the place where they say Paul was imprisoned. It is really just a cold dungeon, a cave in the ground, with bare walls and a little hole in the ceiling where food was dropped down. There were no windows; it was just a cold, little cell that would have been especially uncomfortable in winter.

iii. Paul wrote this letter from his second Roman imprisonment, and soon after he wrote this letter he was condemned and executed in Rome at the command of Nero. Paul sensed this; therefore 2 Timothy is not only the last letter we have from Paul, there is also a note of urgency and passion we might expect from a man who knew he would soon be executed.

2. (2-5) A greeting and a happy remembrance.

To Timothy, a beloved son: Grace, mercy, *and* peace from God the Father and Christ Jesus our Lord. I thank God, whom I serve with a pure conscience, as *my* forefathers *did,* as without ceasing I remember you in my prayers night and day, greatly desiring to see you, being mindful of your tears, that I may be filled with joy, when I call to remembrance the genuine faith that is in you, which dwelt first in your grandmother Lois and your mother Eunice, and I am persuaded is in you also.

a. **To Timothy, a beloved son**: Paul thought much about his spiritual family – about **Timothy, a beloved son**; and about his true **forefathers**, those Jews before Paul's time that genuinely followed God with a pure heart, not in the self-righteousness of the Pharisees.

b. **Grace, mercy, and peace**: Spurgeon used this verse, along with 1 Timothy 1:2 and Titus 1:4 to show that ministers need more **mercy** than others do. After all, in the beginning to his letters to churches in general, Paul only wrote *grace* and *peace* in his greeting (Romans 1:7, 1 Corinthians 1:3, 2 Corinthians 1:2, Galatians 1:3, Ephesians 1:2, Philippians 1:2, Colossians 1:2, 1 Thessalonians 1:1, 2 Thessalonians 1:2). But when he wrote to the pastors – Timothy and Titus – he was compelled to greet them with **grace, mercy, and peace**.

i. "Did you ever notice this one thing about Christian ministers, that they need even more mercy than other people? Although everybody needs mercy, ministers need it more than anybody else; and so we do, for if we are not faithful, we shall be greater sinners even than our hearers, and it needs much grace for us always to be faithful, and much mercy will be required to cover our shortcomings. So I shall take those three things to myself: 'Grace, mercy, and peace.' You may have the two, 'Grace and peace,' but I need mercy more than any of you; so I take it from my Lord's loving hand, and I will trust, and not be afraid, despite all my shortcomings, and feebleness, and blunders, and mistakes, in the course of my whole ministry." (Spurgeon)

c. **Without ceasing I remember you in my prayers night and day**: Timothy was on Paul's prayer list. Paul made it a regular practice to pray with a list and to at least mention in prayer those who were precious to him.

i. **Prayers night and day** also shows how much Paul prayed: Whenever it was **night** or whenever it was **day**. Of course, one might say this was easy for Paul, since he was in prison; but such prayer is never easy.

ii. Paul is to be admired for wanting to do the most for Jesus that he could wherever he was. If he could not preach, then he would pray.

d. **Mindful of your tears**: Perhaps the **tears** Paul remembered were the tears Timothy shed at their last parting.

e. **Filled with joy, when I call to remembrance the genuine faith that is in you**: It made Paul genuinely happy (**filled with joy**) to remember the faith of faithful men like Timothy, who loved and served Jesus and His people.

f. **Which dwelt first in your grandmother Lois and your mother Eunice**: Timothy's **genuine faith** was due, in no small measure, to his godly upbringing and the influence of his grandmother and mother.

i. Timothy and his family came from the ancient city of Lystra, where Paul visited on his first missionary journey (Acts 14:16-20). When Paul and Barnabas were there, God used Paul to miraculously heal a crippled man – and the people of the city began to praise Paul and Barnabas as Greek gods from Olympus, even starting to sacrifice a bull to them. Paul barely restrained them from doing so, and soon enemies of the gospel had turned the crowd against the missionary evangelists, so they cast Paul out of the city and stoned him. Yet God miraculously preserved Paul's life, and he carried on.

ii. On Paul's second missionary journey, he came again to Lystra – and there met a young man who had come to Jesus and was devoted to serving the Lord (Acts 16:1-5). This young man was Timothy, and he is described as having a mother *who believed, but his father was Greek*.

iii. So, Timothy's mother and grandmother were believers, but his father was not (at least not at first). In the Roman world, fathers had absolute authority over the family, and since Timothy's father was not a Christian, his home situation was less than ideal (though not necessarily terrible). But his mother and grandmother either led him to Jesus or grounded him in the faith. God wants to use parents and grandparents to pass on an eternal legacy to their children and grandchildren.

iv. When Paul left Lystra, he took Timothy with him (Acts 16:3-4). This began a mentor-learner relationship that touched the whole world.

g. **I am persuaded is in you also**: It wasn't enough that this **genuine faith** was in Timothy's grandmother and mother; it had to be in Timothy **also**. Our children, once of age to be accountable before God, must have their *own* relationship with Jesus Christ. Mom and dad's relationship with God will not then bring eternal life.

i. The phrase **genuine faith** could be literally translated, *unhypocritical faith* – that is, faith that is not an act. It was for real, not just in appearance. This is a significant theme of the Book of James.

B. Paul exhorts Timothy to be bold.

1. (6) **Stir up the gift of God which is in you**.

Therefore I remind you to stir up the gift of God which is in you through the laying on of my hands.

a. **Therefore I remind you to stir up the gift of God**: Timothy was a gifted, valuable man for the kingdom of God; but he seems to have had a timid streak in him. For this reason, Paul often encouraged him to be strong and bold.

i. It may be that Timothy was somewhat timid, but it is also true that he had large and heavy responsibility as the overseer of God's work in Ephesus and the larger area. There were many Christians in many congregations meeting over a whole region (Acts 19:9-10 and 17-20). Perhaps Timothy was a man of normal courage who had enormous responsibility.

ii. If it was true that Timothy was the kind of man who avoided confrontation, it was good that he saw Paul's example. Paul was a man of deep love, but also a man who never shied away from confrontation. A significant example was when he publicly rebuked the Apostle Peter (Galatians 2:11-21). Timothy already *had* a shepherd's tender heart for the sheep; Paul wanted to develop within him the boldness necessary to really lead and protect the flock.

iii. In 1 and 2 Timothy there are no less than 25 different places where Paul encouraged Timothy to be bold, to not shy away from confrontation, to stand up where he needs to stand up and be strong. Because of who Timothy was and the responsibilities he had to bear, this was what Timothy needed to hear.

b. **Therefore I remind you**: People are at all different places. For some, the last thing they need to hear is, "You need to be bolder" because that is not their problem. Many others come from the place where they need to hear, "**Stir up the gift of God which is in you**; be bold, get going, go for it." Timothy was of this second type.

i. Some who *appear* bold really are just good at pretending. They use a confrontational, in-your-face attitude to mask a lot of pain and insecurity. They need to become really bold and secure *in the Lord*, instead of pretending and hiding behind a mask of false courage.

c. **Stir up the gift of God which is in you**: Timothy could not be passive and just let it all happen; he needed to be bold and to **stir up the gift of God which is in you**. Some have gifts given to them by God, but those gifts are neglected. They need to be stirred up and put into action.

i. This reminds us that God does not work His gifts through us as if we were robots. Even when He gives a man or a woman gifts, He leaves an element that needs the cooperation of their will, of their desire and drive, to fulfill the purpose of His gifts.

ii. Some are waiting passively for God to use them; but God is waiting for them to stir up the gifts that are within them. Some are waiting for some dramatic new anointing from God, and God is waiting for them to stir up what He has already given.

d. **Stir up**: This has the idea of stirring up a fire to keep it burning bright and strong; a fire left to itself will always burn out, but God wants us to keep our gifts burning strong for Him.

i. "The Greek *anazopureo* (*stir up*) means either 'to kindle afresh' or 'to keep in full flame'. There is no necessary suggestion, therefore, that Timothy had lost his early fire, although undoubtedly, like every Christian, he needed an incentive to keep the fire burning at full flame." (Guthrie)

e. **Which is in you through the laying on of my hands**: God used the **laying on of hands** to communicate spiritual gifts to Timothy. This is not the only way God gives gifts, but it is a common way – and a way that we should never neglect. It is a good thing to have others pray for us and as that God would give us gifts that might be used to bless and build up the family of God.

i. "We have no right to assume that hands were laid on Timothy once only. Thus Acts ix. 17 and xiii. 3 are two such occasions in St. Paul's spiritual life. There may have been others." (White)

2. (7) Why Timothy can be bold in using the gifts God has given him: God has given him a spirit of **power and of love and of a sound mind**.

For God has not given us a spirit of fear, but of power and of love and of a sound mind.

a. **God has not given us a spirit of fear**: Paul saw the timidity that was in Timothy; Timothy knew the fear he sometimes felt. God wanted Timothy to know that this fear wasn't from the God he served; he needed to know that **God has not given us a spirit of fear**.

i. We all face situations where we feel timid and afraid. For some, speaking in front of others makes them fear; others are afraid of confrontation, others of being made to look foolish, others are afraid of rejection. We all deal with fear.

ii. The first step in dealing with such fears is to understand that they are *not* from God. It is a significant step to say, "This isn't God making me feel like this; God hasn't given me this." Perhaps it is from personality, perhaps a weakness of the flesh, perhaps a demonic attack – but it isn't from God.

b. **But of power and of love and of a sound mind**: The second step in dealing with such fears is understanding what God *has* given us: a spirit of **power and of love and of a sound mind**.

i. God has given us a spirit of **power**: When we do His work, proclaim His word, represent His kingdom, we have all His power supporting us. We are safe in His hands.

ii. God has given us a spirit of **love**: This tells us a lot about the **power** He has given us. Many think of **power** in terms of how much we can control others; but Jesus' power is expressed in how much we can love and serve others. On the night before the cross, *Jesus, knowing that the Father had given all things into His hands* – and what did He do with all that power? He humbly washed His disciples' feet (John 13:1-11).

iii. God has given us a **sound mind**: The ancient Greek word here had the idea of a calm, self-controlled mind, in contrast to the panic and confusion that comes in a fearful situation.

c. **Not given us a spirit of fear, but of power and of love**: We don't need to accept what God has **not** given us (**a spirit of fear**), and we do need to humbly receive and walk in what He *has* given us (**a spirit… of power and of love and of a sound mind**).

i. Paul wrote this to Timothy because boldness matters; without it, we can't fulfill God's purpose for our lives. God's purpose for is more than making money, being entertained, and being comfortable; it is for each of us to use the gifts He gives to touch His people and help a needy world.

ii. Fear and timidity will keep us from using the gifts God gives. God wants us each to take His power, His love, and His calm thinking and overcome fear, to be used of Him with all the gifts He gives.

3. (8) Using the boldness God gives, don't be ashamed of the imprisoned apostle.

Therefore do not be ashamed of the testimony of our Lord, nor of me His prisoner, but share with me in the sufferings for the gospel according to the power of God.

a. **Therefore**: Paul has just told Timothy about the spirit of power, love, and a sound mind, with courage, that is the birthright of every believer in Jesus Christ. Now he told Timothy *how* to let what God gave him guide his thinking.

b. **Do not be ashamed of the testimony of our Lord**: If Timothy took the courage God gave, he would not be **ashamed of the testimony of our Lord**. We often fail to understand that it wasn't easy to follow a *crucified* Master.

i. Today, we have sanitized Jesus and disinfected the cross, making it all safe. But in the day Paul wrote this, it would seem strange indeed to follow a crucified man and call him savior.

ii. Think of Jesus' teaching; if you want to be great, be the servant of all; be like a child, like a slave, like the younger, like the last instead of the first. This is a testimony some would be **ashamed** of.

iii. Paul knew that the plan of God in Jesus Christ seemed foolish to many; but he also knew it was the living, active, power of God to save souls and transform lives. Paul would not be **ashamed** of it, and neither should Timothy – or us today.

c. **Nor of me His prisoner**: If Timothy took the courage God gave, he would not be ashamed of Paul the **prisoner**. It wasn't easy to support an *imprisoned* apostle.

i. Note that Paul considered himself a prisoner of *Jesus* (**nor of me His prisoner**). Paul saw himself not as the prisoner of Rome, but as a prisoner of God. Paul saw God as the Lord of every circumstance, and if he was free, he was the Lord's free man; if he were imprisoned, he was the Lord's prisoner.

d. **But share with me**: It wasn't enough that Paul told Timothy to not be ashamed of him and his chains; he also invited Timothy to **share** in all of it.

i. We **share... in the sufferings** in the same way Paul spoke of in Romans 12:15: *Rejoice with those who rejoice, and weep with those who weep.* We identify with our suffering brethren across the world through prayer, through a heart of concern, and through wise action.

e. **According to the power of God**: Paul actually suffered **according to the power of God**. The power of God is always there, but it is not always there to *remove* the difficulty. Sometimes it is there to see us *through* the difficulty.

i. In one sense, it was strange for Paul the prisoner to write about the power of God – the power of Rome in some ways seemed a lot more real. But God's power has been vindicated by history; the Roman Empire is gone, but the gospel of Jesus Christ that Paul lived to preach lives on.

4. (9-10) The message Timothy is not to be ashamed of: God's plan of salvation.

Who has saved us and called *us* with a holy calling, not according to our works, but according to His own purpose and grace which was given to us in Christ Jesus before time began, but has now been revealed by the appearing of our Savior Jesus Christ, *who* has abolished death and brought life and immortality to light through the gospel,

a. **Who has saved us and called us**: We come to God as a response to His call in our lives. We did not initiate the search; we do not find God, He finds us; so we must respond to His call when we sense it.

b. **Not according to our works, but according to His own purpose**: This explains *why* God called us. It wasn't anything great we were, or anything great we had done, but because it fit in with His purpose – because He wanted to.

c. **Grace which was given to us in Christ Jesus before time began**: God directed His gracious work towards us when we only existed as a fact in God's knowledge. Just as a couple lovingly plans for a baby before the baby is born, so God planned for us.

i. **Before time began** reminds us that **time** is something God created to give order and arrangement to our present world; time is not essential to God's existence. He existed before time was created and will remain when time ends, and we live on in eternity with Him.

d. **But has now been revealed by the appearing of our Savior Jesus Christ**: The appearing of Jesus revealed the purpose and grace of God. Jesus fulfilled the eternal plan of God; Jesus truly shows us what God and His plan are all about. That's why we can never know Jesus too much.

e. **Who abolished death**: Because of the appearing of Jesus, death isn't death anymore. In regard to believers, it is called **sleep** – not because we are unconscious, but because it is pleasant and peaceful. Death does not *take* anything from the Christian; it graduates them to glory.

i. Someone suggested that the Christian has no place for the letters "RIP" on his tombstone because "Rest in Peace" does not adequately describe our eternal fate. They suggested instead the letters "CAD," signifying "Christ Abolished Death."

f. **And brought life and immortality to light through the gospel**: Because of the appearing of Jesus, we know more about **life and immortality** than before. The understanding of the after-life was murky at best in the Old Testament; but Jesus let us know more about heaven – and hell – than anyone else could.

i. Jesus brought the truth about our immortal state to life through His own resurrection; He showed us what our own immortal bodies would be like and assured us that we would in fact have them. Jesus is therefore a more reliable spokesman regarding the world beyond than anyone who has a near-death experience.

g. **Through the gospel**: The good news of who Jesus is and what He did for us can be thought of as links connected together in a beautiful chain of God's work.

- God's plan of salvation began for us in eternity past, **before time began**.
- It continued with the **appearing of our Savior Jesus Christ**.
- It came to us when He **saved us and called us**.
- It continues as we live our **holy calling**.
- It will one day show itself in **immortality** – eternal life.

i. When we consider the greatness of this message, it is no wonder Paul called it **the gospel** – *good news*. It is good news that God thought of you and loved you before you even existed; good news that Jesus came to perfectly show us God, good news that He called us and saved us, good news that He gives us a holy calling, and good news that He shows us and gives us eternal life.

ii. This message was worth prison to the Apostle Paul.

5. (11-12) Paul's appointed work, and the confidence it gave to him.

To which I was appointed a preacher, an apostle, and a teacher of the Gentiles. For this reason I also suffer these things; nevertheless I am not

ashamed, for I know whom I have believed and am persuaded that He is able to keep what I have committed to Him until that Day.

a. **To which I was appointed a preacher**: We can almost sense Paul growing in strength as he penned these words; he understood again that it was a *privilege* to suffer for such a great gospel – so far from being **ashamed**, he was honored.

> i. Flashing through his mind were the sermons he preached (**a preacher**), the churches he founded and led (**an apostle**), and the diverse nations he brought to Jesus Christ (**a teacher of the Gentiles**). He no doubt thanked Jesus as he considered each one.

b. **For this reason I also suffer these things**: Paul knew that though he preached a wonderful message, it cost him dearly along the way. His present suffering in prion was because of this heavenly appointment.

c. **For I know whom I have believed and am persuaded**: This explains why Paul was so bold in his work, and how he could feel honored by circumstances that might make others feel ashamed. He said that it was because **I know whom I have believed**. Paul knew the God he trusted and served.

> i. We must know *what* we believe; but it is even more important to know **whom** we believe. When we know how great God is; when God and His glory becomes the great fact of our lives, then we have real boldness.

> ii. "'Know thyself,' said the heathen philosopher; that is well, but that knowledge may only lead a man to hell. 'Know Christ,' says the Christian philosopher, 'know him, and then you shall know yourself,' and this shall certainly lead you to heaven, for the knowledge of Christ Jesus is saving knowledge." (Spurgeon)

d. **And am persuaded that He is able to keep what I have committed to Him**: This is a second reason that explains Paul's boldness. Paul gave Jesus his life, and knew Jesus was fully able to keep it!

> i. What was it that Paul **committed to Him**? Surely, he first had in mind *his life*. Paul knew he could not keep his own life; he knew that only God could keep it. God was able; Paul was not. Knowing this made Paul full of boldness, but it wasn't boldness in self, but in God.

> ii. But it wasn't *only* his life that Paul had **committed** to God. Paul had committed everything to Jesus – his life, his body, his character and reputation, his life's work, everything that was precious.

e. **Until that Day**: Paul had in mind either the **Day** he would see Jesus or the **Day** Jesus came for Paul. Paul and Timothy both lived in such awareness of **that Day** that Paul didn't need to identify it more than that.

i. **That Day** was precious to Paul because he had committed everything to Jesus. To the degree we commit our life and all we are and have to Jesus, to that same degree **that Day** will be precious to us.

C. Paul exhorts Timothy to remain faithful to the truth.

1. (13-14) Faithfulness matters, so hold fast the truth.

Hold fast the pattern of sound words which you have heard from me, in faith and love which are in Christ Jesus. That good thing which was committed to you, keep by the Holy Spirit who dwells in us.

a. **Hold fast the pattern of sound words**: After writing of the importance of boldness, Paul next called Timothy (and all godly ministers) to be faithful to God's truth, **the pattern of sound words**.

i. **Hold fast** suggests someone or something would try to take the truth from Timothy. Unless he held on in faithfulness, it would be snatched from him.

ii. It takes a special man or woman to truly **hold fast**; it takes someone who is not *tossed to and fro and carried about by every wind of doctrine, by the trickery of men* (Ephesians 4:14).

iii. This is an important measure for any pastor; he must **hold fast the pattern of sound words**. The primary measure should not be humor or excitement or personality or charisma or even evangelistic interest. Some who claim an evangelistic heart let go of **the pattern of sound words** and show themselves to unfaithful to their Lord and their calling.

b. **The pattern of sound words**: This suggests that true teaching, according to God's truth, has a certain *pattern* – a **pattern** that can be detected by the discerning heart.

c. **Which you have heard from me**: The sound words Timothy was to hold fast came to him from a man – Paul the apostle. God used human instruments to communicate His eternal truth.

i. We must always beware of the person who rejects all human teachers and says, "It's just me and my Bible." God used Paul to communicate **the pattern of sound words**, and Timothy was expected to be faithful to that pattern. God uses other men and women to communicate that same truth today.

d. **In faith and love which are in Christ Jesus**: Timothy's faithfulness has to be tempered with **faith and love which in Christ Jesus**. Some people take God's word and consider it only an intellectual matter, and leave out **faith and love**.

i. **Faith and love** describe how the truth is to be held. We hold it in **faith**, truly believing it and putting our lives on it; and we hold it in **love**, not in proud arrogance or self-seeking superiority.

ii. If one thinks they are faithful to the truth, but do not show **faith** and **love** in the life, they may be nothing more than a Pharisee. They were a group in Jesus' day that was very committed to holding certain teachings, but had no fruit of **faith** and **love** evident in their lives.

e. **That good thing which was committed to you**: Timothy had something **committed** to him – Paul called it **that good thing**, no doubt meaning the gospel and the truth of God. Timothy needed *faithfulness* to **keep** that good thing.

i. God has committed many good things to us; we must be faithful to **keep** them. **Keep** has more than just the idea of holding on to something; it also means to guard it and to use it wisely. God has given us His Word, family relationships, time, talents, resources, education, and so on. We must be faithful to keep those good things in a way that brings glory and credit to Jesus.

ii. We live in a time where faithfulness is only expected so long as it serves our own interests. When it stops being in our immediate advantage to be faithful, many people feel just fine about giving up their responsibility. But this is not honoring to God.

iii. Being faithful to God means having the heart that will to what is right even when it seems not in our advantage to do so. *But he honors those who fear the LORD; he who swears to his own hurt and does not change* (Psalm 15:4). True faithfulness is shown when it *costs* something to be faithful.

iv. God is faithful with what we commit to Him (2 Timothy 1:12). Will we be faithful with what He has committed to us?

f. **Keep by the Holy Spirit who dwells in us**: This is the key to faithfulness. God requires a faithfulness from us that is greater than we can fulfill by our own resources. Unless we walk in the Spirit and are filled with the Holy Spirit, we cannot keep faithful to what we must keep faithful to.

2. (15) An example of unfaithful men.

This you know, that all those in Asia have turned away from me, among whom are Phygellus and Hermogenes.

a. **All those in Asia had turned away from me**: The great apostle Paul, at the end of his days and a fantastic missionary career, was almost all alone. He was not praised by the world, or even regarded much among other Christians.

> i. If there were Christian radio back then, no one would want to interview Paul. If there were Christian magazines back then, Paul would not have been on the cover. Paul would have had a hard time finding a publisher for the books he had written. For many Christians of that day, Paul seemed too extreme, too committed, not flashy or famous enough. Even the Christians of **Asia** – where Paul did a great work (Acts 19) – **turned away** from Paul.

> ii. Geographically, **Asia** in the New Testament doesn't mean the Far Eastern continent as it does today. It means the Roman province of Asia, which today would mostly be Turkey.

b. **Phygellus and Hermogenes**: These were two notable men who among those **turned away** from Paul, were not faithful, and did not *hold fast*.

> i. These two were not the only ones, but Paul found it necessary to point out **Phygellus and Hermogenes** particularly: "He names two of the deserters – probably the best known – in order to put a stop to these slanderous attacks. For it usually happens that deserters from the Christian warfare seek to excuse their own disgraceful conduct by inventing whatever accusations they can against faithful and upright ministers of the gospel" (Calvin).

> ii. We don't know much about **Phygellus and Hermogenes**; this is the only place they are mentioned in the Bible. It's a terrible thing to have your name recorded in God's word as an example of unfaithfulness.

3. (16-18) An example of a faithful man.

The Lord grant mercy to the household of Onesiphorus, for he often refreshed me, and was not ashamed of my chain; but when he arrived in Rome, he sought me out very zealously and found *me*. The Lord grant to him that he may find mercy from the Lord in that Day– and you know very well how many ways he ministered *to me* at Ephesus.

a. **The Lord grant mercy to the household of Onesiphorus**: Onesiphorus was a different sort of man than Phygellus and Hermogenes; he was faithful to Paul in difficult circumstances. Paul therefore prayed for **mercy** on Onesiphorus and his whole household.

i. We don't know much about Onesiphorus, other than that he lived near Timothy, because at the end of the letter Paul asked Timothy to greet Onesiphorus' household.

b. **Onesiphorus**: Paul described many things that made him special.

i. **He often refreshed me**: He was an intentional blessing to Paul, and worked to refresh the apostle who did so much for other people.

ii. **Was not ashamed of my chain**: Onesiphorus showed himself to be a true friend of Paul when the apostle was imprisoned.

iii. **He sought me out very zealously and found me**: There were many prisons in Rome, so it was probably difficult for Onesiphorus to find Paul, but he did.

c. **That he may find mercy from the Lord in that Day**: This was a special prayer for Onesiphorus. If a faithful servant like Onesiphoris needed such a prayer, then all the more do the rest of us.

d. **You know very well**: Apparently, Onesiphorus' service was so faithful, so outstanding, that it was famous – Paul could simply tell Timothy, "**You know very well**" how well he served.

i. Onesiphorus lived up to the meaning of his name, which means "help-bringer."

2 Timothy 2 – Advice to a Young Pastor

A. Working hard for a faithful God.

1. (1) Be strong in grace.

You therefore, my son, be strong in the grace that is in Christ Jesus.

> a. **Be strong**: This was an important encouragement. Paul knew that Timothy would need strength and endurance to fulfill the calling God gave him.

> > i. Again, this is one of the twenty-five times Paul encouraged Timothy to be strong and endure in his work in Ephesus. Perhaps Timothy was naturally timid and easily discouraged, or perhaps he was a man of normal courage who had great responsibilities. He needed to be told often, "**be strong**."

> b. **Be strong**: God is always there to give us strength; *He gives power to the weak, and to those who have no might, He increases strength… those that wait on the LORD shall renew their strength* (Isaiah 40:29, 31). However, we must *receive* this strength, therefore Paul had to encourage Timothy to **be strong**.

> > i. God makes the resource of His strength available to us (Ephesians 6:10-11). Yet it does not come as we sit back passively and suppose that God will simply pour it into us. He brings His strength to us as we seek Him and rely on Him instead of our own strength.

> c. **Be strong in the grace that is in Christ Jesus**: Paul told Timothy a *specific way to be strong* – that is, to be **strong in the grace that is in Christ Jesus**. This strength in **grace** is essential for a strong Christian life.

> > i. "*Grace* here has its simplest theological meaning, as the divine help, the unmerited gift of assistance that comes from God" (White). Resting in the **grace** – the *unmerited favor of God towards us that is in Christ Jesus* – gives a confidence and boldness we could never have

when thinking we are on probation or thinking God hasn't made up His mind about us yet.

ii. There is nothing that can makes us as strong as saying, "I am a child of God in Jesus Christ" and "I have the love and favor of God even though I don't deserve it." That is the strength that comes by grace.

iii. Paul knew what it was like to receive the strength of God's grace, as he explained in 2 Corinthians 12:9-10: *And He said to me, "My grace is sufficient for you, for My strength is made perfect in weakness." Therefore most gladly I will rather boast in my infirmities, that the power of Christ may rest upon me.* He could encourage Timothy like this from his own life experience.

2. (2) Spread the word among faithful men.

And the things that you have heard from me among many witnesses, commit these to faithful men who will be able to teach others also.

a. **The things that you have heard from me among many witnesses**: Paul reminded Timothy of the body of truth that he had heard from the Apostle in the presence of many others. Certainly, Timothy heard many Bible studies from Paul, and shared much time with the Apostle in personal discipleship.

i. It may be that Paul reminded Timothy of a special message he presented at Timothy's ordination service **among many witnesses**. "But he seems to refer here to the doctrines delivered to him when, in the *presence of many witnesses*, he laid his hands upon him; see 1 Timothy 6:12. Then the apostle gave him the proper form of sound words which he was to teach; and now he tells him to commit those truths to faithful men in the say way that they were committed to him" (Clarke).

b. **Commit these to faithful men**: God gave ministry to Timothy, not for him to keep to himself, but for him to pass on to others. An essential part of his work as a pastor was to pour into others what God had committed to him.

i. One may say that everything that a pastor does in his ministry he should train others to do. There are no duties of a pastor so holy or so secret that he should keep them all to himself. He should always seek to spread ministry about to others, and to train others to do the work of the ministry.

ii. Timothy was not to teach others his own particular ideas or theories, but simple apostolic doctrine and example (**the things that you have**

heard from me). What Paul poured into him he was responsible to pour into others.

iii. The job of training leaders is simply part of a pastor's job description. He should not only train leaders when the need for a leader is obvious; nor should he only train leaders for the needs of his congregation alone. He should train leaders for the Kingdom of God in general, whether they are used in ministry at the particular pastor's congregation or not.

c. **To faithful men**: When Timothy looked for those whom he could pour apostolic doctrine and practice into, he was to look for the quality of *faithfulness*. He didn't need to find smart men, popular men, strong men, easy men, perfect men, or good-looking men; Paul told him to look for **faithful men**.

i. Through the history of Christianity, some have held to the idea of *apostolic succession*. This is the idea that you can know who a true minister of the gospel is because Peter ordained someone to succeed him, and that one ordained someone to succeed him, and the next one ordained someone to succeed him, so forth and so on down the line. However, this verse reveals the real apostolic succession – the succession of **faithful men**, who take the teachings of the apostles and pass them on.

ii. Without faithfulness to the teaching and example of the apostles, the idea of apostolic succession is nothing more than the laying of empty hands upon empty heads. "Where is the *uninterrupted* apostolic succession? Who can tell? Probably it does not exist on the face of the world. All the pretensions to it by certain Churches are as stupid as they are idle and futile" (Clarke).

d. **Who will be able to teach others also**: This job of training leaders was so important that it could not be restricted to Timothy alone. Those whom he had trained must also be given the job to **teach others also**.

i. **Will be able** "Expresses capability as proved by experience" (White).

3. (3-4) Persevere for God with a soldier's attitude.

You therefore must endure hardship as a good soldier of Jesus Christ. No one engaged in warfare entangles himself with the affairs of *this* life, that he may please him who enlisted him as a soldier.

a. **You therefore must**: This was not a suggestion from Paul to Timothy; **must** carries the sense of a requirement or a command. There was something that Timothy had to do, and Paul would tell him to do it.

b. **Endure hardship as a good solider**: Timothy **must** take the attitude of soldier who *expects* to **endure hardship** for their cause. No real solider – or at least no good solider – ever gave up simply because some hardship came to them.

> i. In the same way, if a believer is not willing to endure hardship, they will never accomplish much for Jesus Christ. They will give up as soon as something hard is required of them; they cannot fulfill Jesus' call: *If anyone desires to come after Me, let him deny himself, and take up his cross, and follow Me.* (Matthew 16:24)

> ii. "Never dream of delicacy; think not to find God in the gardens of Egypt, whom Moses found not but in the burning-bush." (Trapp)

> iii. "Paul does not exhort Timothy to be a common, or ordinary soldier, but to be a 'good soldier of Jesus Christ;' for all soldiers, and all true soldiers, may not be good soldiers. There are men who are but just soldiers and nothing more; they only need sufficient temptation and they readily become cowardly, idle, useless and worthless; but he is the good soldier who is bravest of the brave, courageous at all times, who is zealous, does his duty with heart and earnestness." (Spurgeon)

c. **No one engaged in warfare entangles himself with the affairs of this life**: Timothy must take the attitude of a solider, who willingly separates himself from the things of civilian life.

> i. A solider has to give up many things. Some of them are bad things (pride, independence, self-will), and some of them are good things (his home, his family). Nevertheless, if a soldier is not willing to give up these things, he is not a soldier at all.

> ii. The things that might *entangle* a soldier might be good or bad for a civilian. The soldier can't ask if something is good or bad for those who are not soldiers; he must give up anything that gets in the way of being a good soldier or serving his commanding officer. A faithful soldier does not have the right to do anything that will entangle them and make them less effective as a soldier.

> iii. "It is well remarked by *Grotius*, on this passage, that the legionary soldiers among the Romans were not permitted to engage in husbandry, merchandise, mechanical employments, or any thing that might be inconsistent with their calling." (Clarke)

d. **That he may please him who enlisted him as a soldier**: If Timothy did not endure hardship and if he did not put away the things that entangled him in the affairs of this life, he would not be pleasing to his Commanding Officer.

i. Jesus Christ is the commander of all heaven's armies. In Joshua 5, Jesus appeared to Joshua as *Commander of the army of the* LORD (Joshua 5:14). He is our Commanding Officer, and we owe total obedience to Him as such.

ii. It is likely that Paul was chained to a soldier even as he wrote this. He saw how these soldiers acted, and how they obeyed their commanding officers. Paul knew that this is how a Christian must act towards their Lord.

4. (5) Persevere for God with an athlete's attitude.

And also if anyone competes in athletics, he is not crowned unless he competes according to the rules.

a. **If anyone competes in athletics**: Paul often drew upon the world of athletics for illustrations of the Christian life, mentioning track and field (1 Corinthians 9:12), boxing (1 Corinthians 9:26), and wrestling (Ephesians 6:12).

b. **He is not crowned unless he competes according to the rules**: The point is clear. An athlete can't make up the rules as he pleases; he must compete **according to the rules** if he wants to receive the crown.

i. It is possible to fall into the mistake of thinking that we can make up our own rules for our Christian life. For some people, their special arrangement goes something like this: "I know this is sin, but God *understands*, so I'll just keep going in this sin." This goes against the attitude of an athlete who must compete according to the rules.

5. (6) Persevere for God with the attitude of a farmer.

The hard-working farmer must be first to partake of the crops.

a. **The hard-working farmer**: In calling Timothy to have the attitude of a farmer, Paul emphasized the fact that farmers are **hard-working**. In the same way, all who serve the Lord should be **hard-working**.

i. Unlike the soldier and the athlete, there is nothing glamorous about the work a farmer does. It is often tedious, boring, and unexciting. The nation's best farmer really isn't a celebrity. But he must work hard just the same.

ii. God has no place for lazy ministers. If you will not work hard, get out of the ministry. If you will only work hard if you are in the limelight, then let God change your heart.

iii. "Idle drones disgrace every department of the Christian Church. They cannot teach because they will not learn." (Clarke)

b. **Hard-working**: Paul knew the value of hard work. He could say, comparing himself with the other apostles, *I labored more abundantly than they all* (1 Corinthians 15:10). Paul wasn't just called, he wasn't just blessed, he wasn't just anointed; Paul was also **hard-working**. His ministry would have been far less than it was if he had *not* worked hard.

i. Some people expect something for nothing. But wise people know that you often get out of things according to the measure you put into them. If you are putting forth little effort in your Christian walk, you should expect little result.

ii. Yet at the same time, Paul knew that all the work he did was the gift of God's grace in him: *I labored more abundantly than they all, yet not I, but the grace of God which was with me* (1 Corinthians 15:10). Paul knew the balance of working hard, yet always knowing it is all of grace.

c. **Must be the first to partake of the crops**: When Timothy had spiritual food to give to the congregation, he must eat of it first. If he wasn't being fed from the Word of God, he couldn't really feed others.

i. An effective pastor or teacher will get more out of the message than the audience does, and his time of preparation to teach God's word will also be a time of warm fellowship with God.

d. **Partake of the crops**: Like a good farmer, any godly pastor will work hard and he will patiently await the harvest – which really comes at the end of the age, not at the end of the meeting.

6. (7) Looking to the Lord for **understanding**.

Consider what I say, and may the Lord give you understanding in all things.

a. **Consider what I say**: Paul has just explained three illustrations of the Christian life – a soldier, an athlete, and a farmer. Each of these three occupations need great *perseverance* to succeed.

- The solider who stops fighting before the battle is finished will never see victory.
- The athlete who stops running before the race is over will never win the race.
- The farmer who stops working before the harvest is complete will never see the fruit of his crops.

b. **May the Lord give you understanding in all things**: Timothy was instructed to see the importance of perseverance, and to receive **understanding** from the Lord in all these things.

i. God is faithful **give** us **understanding** in all these things, and He will be faithful to give us the grace to *be strong*. God gives this and we must receive it.

B. Holding steadfast to the truth.

1. (8) The content of Paul's gospel.

Remember that Jesus Christ, of the seed of David, was raised from the dead according to my gospel.

a. **Remember**: Paul did not give this warning because it was something Timothy might easily forget. He said it because Timothy needed to be reminded to keep this in the forefront of his message.

b. **Jesus Christ, of the seed of David**: Timothy needed to keep the fact that Jesus was the Messiah of Israel – the **seed of David** – in the forefront of his preaching.

i. God's plan of rescue through Jesus Christ did not begin when the baby was born in Bethlehem. All of history looked forward to what Jesus would do to save us.

c. **Who was raised from the dead**: This is the great fact, the great credential of the authenticity of Jesus Christ – His resurrection from the dead.

i. Remember that Jesus was the first one ever resurrected. Others, such as Jesus' friend Lazarus, had been *resuscitated*, but only Jesus had been *resurrected* – raised to a new order of life, with a new body, which though based on the old, was still new and fitted for the glories of eternal life.

ii. Jesus' resurrection was the proof that though it looked like He died on the cross as a common criminal, He actually died as a sinless man, giving His life out of love and self-sacrifice to bear the guilt of our sin. Jesus' death on the cross was the payment but the resurrection was the receipt, showing that the payment was received as perfect before God the Father.

d. **Of the seed of David**: This statement means that Jesus was fully man; **raised from the dead** means Jesus was fully God. For Paul, it was essential that Timothy remember and teach the truth about who Jesus was.

e. **According to my gospel**: Of course, the gospel belonged to Paul in the sense that he preached it; but it also belonged to him in the sense that he believed it. It was *his* gospel and it should also be the gospel of each individual Christian.

i. Remember what the word **gospel** means: *good news*. For Paul, the best news was not about more money, more love, more status, or more stuff. The good news was about a real relationship with God through the finished work of Jesus Christ on the cross.

2. (9) The consequences of Paul's gospel.

For which I suffer trouble as an evildoer, *even* **to the point of chains; but the word of God is not chained.**

a. **For which I suffer**: This gospel did not bring Paul a life of glamour and ease. It brought him a life full of adventure and challenge, and a life also marked by suffering.

> i. It was around the time Paul wrote 2 Timothy that a terrible fire destroyed much of Rome, a fire that was reportedly set by the emperor Nero as the first step of his own peculiar urban renewal program. The fire destroyed vast neighborhoods of the poor, and when they rioted, Nero blamed the Christians. He then arrested many of them – perhaps including Paul.

> ii. One of the most spectacular sights in Israel is the ancient city of Beit She'an – a spectacular city that is, piece by piece, being uncovered and restored by archaeologists. If you ever visit, you can see the coliseum there – the oval stadium, complete with chambers and rooms for lions and other wild animals – animals that were almost certainly set upon Christians for the entertainment of the mob. For me, to walk on floor of that stadium – on the ground that had almost surely received the blood of Christians – was something sacred, and reminded me of the extreme price many have had to pay. In the modern western world, the price we pay for faithfulness to Jesus seems small in comparison.

> iii. Any true follower of Jesus Christ will be willing to suffer with Him. Those who are determined to never suffer for Jesus may admire Him from a distance, but they do not genuinely follow Him.

b. **To the point of chains; but the word of God is not chained**: Paul's wrist was shackled at the very moment he wrote this. Nevertheless, he understood that they could chain him but they could never chain **the word of God**.

> i. The Bible has been attacked more than any other book through history. It has been burned, banned, mocked, twisted, and ignored – but the word of God still stands forever. *The grass withers, the flower fades, but the word of our God stands forever* (Isaiah 40:8).

> ii. **The word of God is not chained**. No government, no religious authorities, no skeptics, no scientists, no philosophers, or no book burners have ever been able to stop the work of the Word of God. Yet, if there is any sense in which the Word is bound, it is bound when its

supposed friends abandon it. When pulpits sound more like self-help books than those who proclaim God's word; when Scripture is used sparingly like a spice in a message, instead of being the core of it, pastors themselves put a chain around the Bible.

3. (10) Why Paul endures the consequences of the gospel.

Therefore I endure all things for the sake of the elect, that they also may obtain the salvation which is in Christ Jesus with eternal glory.

a. **Therefore I endure all things for the sake of the elect**: We might have expected Paul to say he endures all things for the sake of God. Yet Paul knew that his love for God could reliably be measured by his love for God's people.

i. "St. Paul was much sustained by the thought that his labours and sufferings were, in the providence of God, beneficial to others." (White)

b. **That they may obtain the salvation**: Paul's life was not spent merely in getting people rescued in Jesus, but also in seeing them grow and become complete in their relationship with Him.

c. **Eternal glory**: The idea of **eternal glory** is hard for us to comprehend. The Bible tells us there is a glory that belongs to the people of God in eternity that is greater than any earthly glory. **Eternal glory** is worth much more than earthly glory.

4. (11-13) Paul describes his gospel with a **faithful saying**.

This is **a faithful saying:**
For if we died with *Him*,
We shall also live with *Him*
If we endure, we shall also reign with *Him*.
If we deny *Him*,
He also will deny us.
If we are faithless,
He remains faithful;
He cannot deny Himself.

a. **This is a faithful saying**: We know what it is like to have a worship song on our mind, one that expressing our heart. Here Paul quoted an early Christian hymn known among the Christians of his day.

b. **For if we died with Him, we shall also live with Him**: The song begins with a promise of resurrection to those who have died with Jesus.

i. The Bible speaks of dying with Jesus in at least two ways.

• The first is common to all Christians, and is illustrated by baptism (Romans 6:3-5). Each of us can have a life-after-death experience with Jesus, seeing our old life ended with Jesus on the cross, and have our new life beginning with His being raised from the dead.

- The other way the Bible speaks of dying with Jesus is, of course, in the sense of martyrdom – of paying the ultimate price for following Jesus. This is probably Paul's idea here; he is saying, "If we die with Him, we aren't dead – we live with Him." More significantly, Paul wrote this awaiting his own execution by the Roman government.

ii. "The context here seems rather to point to physical death as the highest point of suffering for Christ. The reference then is to the martyr's death now viewed from the standpoint of the crowning day." (Hiebert)

c. **If we endure, we shall also reign with Him**: The song assures the faithful believer of eternal reward. This principle assures us that our present difficulty or trial is worth enduring. The reward is greater than what one might gain from quitting. We will **reign with Him**!

i. The Bible says that we will rule and reign with Jesus Christ. This future destiny explains much of the difficulty described in this passage. We understand that God is training us to rule and reign beside Him in the world to come.

d. **If we deny Him, He also will deny us**: The song warns those who deny Jesus that they themselves will be denied. By doctrine or manner of living, one may deny who Jesus is, deny what He has done for us, or deny what He commands us to do.

i. Jesus said it plainly: *But whoever denies Me before men, him I will also deny before My Father who is in heaven.* (Matthew 10:33)

e. **If we are faithless, He remains faithful**: We cannot deny Jesus and we must keep our allegiance to Him. Yet if one does fall away, it doesn't change who God is – **He remains faithful**.

i. It is a terrible thing when people who name the name of Jesus show themselves unfaithful; many have been turned off from Jesus because of the hypocrisy of those who take His name. But all the *faithlessness* of man doesn't disprove the *faithfulness* of God.

ii. "Our faithlessness cannot in any way detract from the Son of God and His Glory. Being all sufficient in Himself He has no need of our confession. It is as if he had said, 'Let all who will desert Christ, for they deprive him of nothing; when they perish, He remains unchanged.'" (Calvin)

iii. But the Christian can stand faithful as God empowers them. Even if one has been wavering, they still have time – as the Spirit of God calls to them even now – to turn back to the faithful God. We can be like the prodigal son, who came to his senses, saw his faithfulness, and came home to his father who had been faithful to him the whole time.

iv. When one Christian in the days of the ancient Roman Empire was commanded to give money to the building of a pagan temple, he refused; and though he was old, they stripped him practically naked, and cut him all over his body with knives and spears. They started to feel sorry for him, so they said, "Just give one dollar to the building of the temple." But he still would not. "Just burn one grain of incense to this pagan god," they asked – but he would not. So, he was smeared with honey, and while his wounds were still bleeding, they set bees and wasps upon him until he was stung to death. He could die; but he could not deny his Lord. The Lord can give you the same strength to live for Him, even as this man died for Him.

C. Keeping attention on the most important things.

1. (14) Keep focused; don't be distracted by unprofitable things.

Remind *them* of these things, charging *them* before the Lord not to strive about words to no profit, to the ruin of the hearers.

a. **Remind them of these things**: After reminding Timothy of the essential points of the gospel, Paul added that Timothy must always **remind** his hearers of **these things**. Timothy's job as a pastor was to keep his congregation always focused on the gospel.

i. The church is constantly tempted to get its focus off of the message that really matters, and is tempted to become an entertainment center, a social service agency, a mutual admiration society, or any number of other things. But this temptation must be resisted, and the church should constantly remember **these things**.

- The things of 2 Timothy 2:8: *Remember that Jesus Christ, of the seed of David, was raised from the dead according to my gospel.*

- The things of 2 Timothy 2:11-13: *For if we died with Him, we shall also live with Him. If we deny Him, He will also deny us. If we are faithless, He remains faithful, He cannot deny Himself.*

b. **Not to strive about words to no profit**: At the same time, there were things that Timothy must *not* focus on. The church must stand for the truth, but it must not become a debating society.

i. We can get distracted by endless discussion or strife over things that don't have central importance. "Words, not *things*, have been a most fruitful source of contention in the Christian world; and among religious people, the principle cause of animosity has arisen from the *different manner* of apprehending the same *term*, while, in *essence*, both meant the *same thing*." (Clarke)

ii. "Let us notice first that teaching is rightly condemned on the sole ground that it does no good. God's purpose is not to pander to our inquisitiveness but to give us profitable instruction. Away with all speculations that produce no edification!" (Calvin)

c. **To the ruin of the hearers**: This shows that it is a serious matter and there is much to lose. If we take the focus off the message of God and put the focus on human opinions and endless debates, it will result in **the ruin of the hearers**.

i. The Bible says, *faith comes by hearing, and hearing by the word of God* (Romans 10:17). Yet if people do not hear the word of God, then **ruin** comes by hearing the opinions and speculations and entertainment of man.

2. (15) Keep focused; pay attention to your own life and ministry.

Be diligent to present yourself approved to God, a worker who does not need to be ashamed, rightly dividing the word of truth.

a. **Be diligent**: Paul often had to exhort Timothy to courage and action. Earlier in the chapter (2 Timothy 2:3-5), Paul encouraged him to hard work and endurance for the service of the Lord.

b. **To present yourself approved to God**: Timothy's goal was not to present himself approved to *people*, but **to God**. He wasn't to regard the job of being a pastor as a popularity contest but instead as a call to faithfulness **to God**.

c. **To present yourself approved to God**: Timothy wasn't to worry so much about presenting other people approved to God (though there was a place for this in his pastoral ministry). His first concern had to be to present *himself* approved to God.

d. **A worker who does not need to be ashamed**: It is embarrassing to do a job poorly and then to have your work examined. The Bible warns us that the work of each Christian will be examined at the judgment seat of Christ (2 Corinthians 5:10). Therefore, we have another motivation to work diligently for the Lord, so we will not be **ashamed** when our work is examined.

i. "It is better explained as *a workman who has no cause for shame when his work is being inspected.*" (White)

e. **Rightly dividing the word of truth**: This was to be a focus of Timothy's hard work. He was to work hard so he could rightly divide the word of God.

i. Timothy, as a faithful pastor, was to be **rightly dividing** God's Word. That is, he had to know what it said and didn't say, and how it was to be understood and how it was not to be understood. It wasn't enough for Timothy to know some Bible stories and verses and sprinkle them through his sermons as illustrations. His teaching was to be a "right dividing" of the Word of God, correctly teaching his congregation.

ii. "Swords are meant to cut and hack, and wound, and kill with, and the word of truth is for pricking men in the heart and killing their sins. The word of God is not committed to God's ministers to amuse men with its glitter, nor to charm them with the jewels in its hilt, but to conquer their souls for Jesus." (Spurgeon)

iii. **Rightly dividing** has several ideas associated with the ancient term.

- *Rightly handle* the Word of God, as one would rightly handle a sword.
- *Plow straight* with the Word of God, properly presenting the essential doctrines.
- *Properly dissect and arrange* the Word of God, as a priest would dissect and arrange and animal for sacrifice.
- *Allot to each their portion*, as someone distributing food at a table.

f. **Rightly dividing**: This also means there is such a thing as *wrongly dividing*; not everyone cuts it straight. We must understand that Biblical truth is not just an issue left up to everyone's interpretation. There is a right way and a wrong way to understand the Bible, and a pastor especially must work hard to master the right interpretation.

i. For example, many people love to say when the Bible is quoted, "Well, that's just your interpretation." Their idea is, "You interpret the Bible your way, I interpret it my way, and another person interprets it their way. We can never really know what it means, so don't judge me with your Bible verse."

ii. When someone tells me, "That's just your interpretation," I think in response: "It's true that it is *my* interpretation, but it isn't *just* my interpretation, it is the *correct* interpretation, and we need to pay attention to what the Bible says correctly interpreted."

iii. This is an important point: The Bible *does not* mean just what anyone wants it to mean. There may be many people trying to twist the Scriptures to their own ends, but they are *wrongly* **dividing the word of truth**. We can't just pick the interpretation that seems most comfortable to us and claim it as true – it must be **rightly dividing the word of truth**, and it must be consistent with what the Bible says in the specific passage and with the entire message of the Scriptures.

iv. For example, a *correct* interpretation of Matthew 7:1 (*Judge not, that you be not judged*) is not the idea of "You have no right to judge my behavior or anyone else's behavior." If this were the case, then Jesus *repeatedly* broke His own commandment because He often told people their behavior was wrong in the sight of God. The correct understanding of Matthew 7:1 is easily seen by reading Matthew 7:2: *For with what judgment you judge, you will be judged; and with the same measure you use, it will be measured back to you.* Jesus was saying "Don't judge anyone by a standard you are not willing to be judged by. God will hold you to the same standard you hold others to." This *clearly* does not forbid judging someone else's life, but it does prohibit doing it unfairly or hypocritically, or living with a judgmental attitude.

v. The point is clear: There is a *right* way and a *wrong* way to divide the Matthew 7:1, which is one verse in the word of truth. Every Christian, but pastors especially, must *work hard* to be **rightly dividing the word of truth**. Though *perfection* in understanding God's word is impossible, and should never be assumed, we should still work hard at it.

3. (16-18) The price of not keeping focus: The faith of some is overthrown.

But shun profane *and* idle babblings, for they will increase to more ungodliness. And their message will spread like cancer. Hymenaeus and Philetus are of this sort, who have strayed concerning the truth, saying that the resurrection is already past; and they overthrow the faith of some.

a. **But shun profane and idle babblings**: This refers to anything that takes the focus off of the gospel and God's Word. These **babblings** are **profane** because they are unholy in contrast to the holiness of God's Word. They are **idle**, because even though people like to hear them, they don't have lasting value.

i. Man's opinions, man's teachings, man's opinion polls, man's stories, man's programs, are all **profane and idle babblings** compared to the simple Word of God. When these things become the focus of the message from the pulpit, it will **increase to more ungodliness**.

b. **Their message will spread like cancer**: The message of **profane and idle babblings** may spread quickly and be popular. They are like a cancer that spreads fast and captures an audience.

i. **Who** in 2 Timothy 2:18 "Implies that Hymenaeus and Philetus were only the more conspicuous members of a class of false teachers." (White)

c. **Hymenaeus and Philetus**: Hymenaeus is mentioned in 1 Timothy 1:20 as a man whom Paul *delivered to Satan that* [he] *may learn not to blaspheme.* This is the only place where we hear of Philetus, and here Paul tells us of their error.

i. They were **of this sort** – that is, they had a message full of **profane and idle babblings**, and apparently the message was somewhat popular, because it spread quickly.

ii. They had **strayed concerning the truth**: Apparently, they started out correctly, and then **strayed** from that correct position.

iii. They were **saying that the resurrection is already past**: It seems they were teaching that we were already in God's millennial kingdom, or that there was no resurrection to come – it had already occurred.

iv. They did **overthrow the faith of some**: Though the only false doctrine Paul mentioned regarding these two is that they taught that **the resurrection is already past**, the effect was to **overthrow the faith of some**. Undoubtedly, this was not their *only* error; and a fundamental error in such an area often leads to many more strange beliefs, until one has abandoned Jesus and His truth all together.

v. Many today accept and honor teachers who are way off in one area or another; and they justify it by saying, "I eat the meat and spit out the bones." This kind of thinking will *certainly* **overthrow the faith of some** because some will *certainly* choke to spiritual death on the bones you say you spit out.

vi. Notice Paul said, **they overthrow the faith of *some***. We shouldn't require that *everyone* be led astray by a teacher before we avoid them; even if *some* are having their faith overthrown, it is bad enough.

4. (19) The reward of focus: **The solid foundation of God.**

Nevertheless the solid foundation of God stands, having this seal: "The Lord knows those who are His," and, "Let everyone who names the name of Christ depart from iniquity."

a. **Nevertheless, the solid foundation of God stands**: In the preceding passage, Paul sounded as if he were under severe attack and might not stand against the rising tide of deception and wickedness. But here, he makes it clear, both to himself and to us that the kingdom of God cannot be shaken.

i. Though men like Hymenaeus and Philetus made dangerous attacks against the church and their message spread like cancer, and even though the faith of some might be overthrown, **nevertheless, the solid foundation of God stands**.

ii. God has a plan, God has a purpose, God has a strategy, and it is not going to fail. It doesn't matter how many fall away, how many reject the truth, how many go their own way after *profane and vain babblings* – **Nevertheless, the solid foundation of God stands**.

b. **Having this seal**: There are two seals on the solid foundation of God. "The one seal bears two inscriptions, two mutually complementary parts or aspects." (White)

i. It seems that Paul drew these allusions from Numbers 16, in reference to the rebellion of Korah.

- **The Lord knows those who are His**: "The words are taken from Numbers 16:5, 'In the morning the Lord will show who are His.'" (White)

- **Let everyone who names the name of Christ depart from iniquity**: "The language is perhaps another echo of the story of Korah (Numbers 16:26-27). But Isaiah 52:11 is nearer in sentiment." (White)

c. **The Lord knows those who are His**: This is the first inscription on the seal. If Hymenaeus and Philetus continue their destructive ministry, **the Lord knows those who are His**. If profane and vain babblings sweep through the church like cancer, **the Lord knows those who are His**. If the faith of some is overthrown, **the Lord knows those who are His**.

i. *We* don't always know **those who are His**. We can know for ourselves, for as Romans 8:16 says, *The Spirit Himself bears witness with our spirit that we are children of God*. But with others, we cannot always know **those who are His**.

ii. God does not sit in heaven, wondering and worrying if you are saved or not. He does not hope or wonder if you will make it to the end. He knows. **The Lord knows those who are His**.

d. **Let everyone who names the name of Christ depart from iniquity**: This is the second inscription on the foundation of God. It is true that God knows those who are His; and He calls those who are His to leave their sin behind.

i. Some might say, "I belong to the Lord, I know I'm His. I am going to heaven. It doesn't matter so much how I live." Yet, such a son has forgotten that there are *two* inscriptions on the foundation of God. There are *two* – and those who **are His** will have the desires and the actions to **depart from iniquity**.

ii. If someone does not have the desire or the actions to **depart from iniquity**, it is fair to ask if they really belong to Jesus or if they have just deceived themselves.

e. **The solid foundation of God stands**: It isn't going to change; therefore, we can keep our focus on it. It is hard to focus on something that often changes, so God gave us a solid foundation in His Word to keep our focus on.

i. "The first seal marked it for the Lord, the second secured its removal from the common stones around it. First comes election, and sanctification follows. I want every professing Christian to have that double mark, and so to be Christ's man, known of all to be such by coming out from the unclean, and being separated unto the Lord." (Spurgeon)

D. Living your life and being used by God.

1. (20-21) Vessels of honor and dishonor.

But in a great house there are not only vessels of gold and silver, but also of wood and clay, some for honor and some for dishonor. Therefore if anyone cleanses himself from the latter, he will be a vessel for honor, sanctified and useful for the Master, prepared for every good work.

a. **But in a great house**: Paul just used the picture of God's building (*the solid foundation of God stands*). Now he thinks of that building as a **great house** that has a variety of **vessels** in it – bowls, plates, vases, and other such things.

i. The church of God is indeed a **great house**.

- It is a **great house** because of *who it belongs to*. The house of our great God is certainly a **great house.**

- It is a **great house** because it is planned and designed on a great scale. It has the most brilliant Architect and houses a great multitude of the greatest people to ever walk the earth.

- It is a **great house** because of the great cost it took to build it. This is a mansion far more valuable than any real estate on earth, built by the great work of Jesus on the cross.

- It is a **great house** because of its importance. This house and what happens in it is at the center of God's plan of the ages. The business of this house is more important than any of the trivia most of the world is interested it.

b. **Vessels of gold and silver, but also of wood and clay**: Some of these **vessels** are made of **gold and silver**, and some are made of **wood and clay**. Some are used on occasions of great **honor** (the gold and silver vessels), and some are used for **dishonor** – such as a garbage bin or an ashtray.

c. **Therefore, if anyone cleanses himself from the latter**: The **latter** things are the things of **dishonor** mentioned in 2 Timothy 2:20. If we cleanse ourselves from dishonorable things, God will regard us as **vessels of honor, sanctified and useful for the Master**.

d. **If anyone cleanses himself**: Paul spoke about a cleansing that isn't just something God does for us as we sit passively. This is a *self-cleansing for service* that goes beyond a general cleansing for sin.

　　i. There is a main aspect of cleansing which comes to us as we trust in Jesus and His work on our behalf. This work of cleansing is really God's work in us and not our work. This is the sense of 1 John 1:9: *If we confess our sins, He is faithful and just to forgive us our sins and to cleanse us from all unrighteousness.*

　　ii. But there is another aspect of cleansing which God looks for us to do with the participation of our own will and effort. Not that it is our work apart from God, but it is a work that awaits our will and effort: **If anyone cleanses himself**. This aspect of cleansing is mostly connected with usefulness for service, and closeness to God.

　　iii. "Oh, happy be you that you be now in this scouring-house; for shortly you shall be set upon the celestial shelf as bright as angels." (Trapp)

e. **Sanctified and useful**: **Sanctified** means *set apart*, just as much as there are certain bowls and plates that we use more than others, or are set aside to some honorable purpose, so some people are more **sanctified and useful** to God than others. They are more **prepared for every good work** than others.

　　i. We must never think that some Christians are better than others, or that some have passed into a place where they are super-spiritual. However, we must also realize that some Christians *are* more able to be used by God than others, because they have cleansed themselves, and made themselves more usable to God.

f. **Prepared for every good work**: We must not think of being usable primarily in the sense of serving in the church. God wants to use His people for **every good work**, including those at the workplace, the school, in the home, in the community. This happens as one will cleanse himself and set yourself aside to God as a **vessel for honor**.

i. There is a large sense in which it is left to us how we want to be used by God. We have the potential to be used as a **vessel of honor** or as a vessel of **dishonor**. According to this picture, we could be a gold platter in the house of God, beautifully displaying the fruit of the Spirit. Or we could be an ashtray or a garbage can in God's house.

ii. Your conduct – clean or unclean; set apart to God or not set apart to God; useful to Jesus or not useful to Jesus – really matters. It greatly effects how God can use you and will use you to touch the lives of others.

2. (22-23) How to cleanse yourself.

Flee also youthful lusts; but pursue righteousness, faith, love, peace with those who call on the Lord out of a pure heart. But avoid foolish and ignorant disputes, knowing that they generate strife.

a. **Flee also youthful lusts**: This is the first aspect of cleansing that Paul mentioned to Timothy. **Youthful lusts** describe the sort of desires and temptations that are especially prominent when someone is an adolescent or young adult. Sexual temptation, illicit pleasure of the flesh, and a longing for fame and glory often mark one's youth.

i. The command is simple: **Flee also youthful lusts**. Don't entertain them. Don't challenge them. Don't try and endure them. The idea of "I will just test myself on this one to see if I can stand against it" has made many fall into sin.

ii. If you cannot **flee also youthful lusts**, there is a real limit to how much God can use you, a limit to how *useful to the Master* you will be. You can't really say "yes" to God until you can say "no" to some other things.

iii. "He has just been cautioned against the errors of the intellect; he must be warned also against vices of the blood." (White)

b. **But pursue righteousness, faith, love, peace**: Cleansing can never be a matter of just avoiding bad things. It must also be the pursuit of good things. Therefore, there are both things that we must **flee** from and things we must **pursue**.

c. **Pursue... peace with those who call on the Lord out of a pure heart**: To be cleansed, we must do everything we can to be right in our personal relationships with others. Cleansing needs to extend to how we treat others.

i. Sometimes relationships are not right with others, but we have done all we can do to set it right. We must take great care that we do all we can do. As Paul wrote in Romans 12:18: *If it is possible, as much as depends on you, live peaceably with all men.*

ii. Bad relationships really hinder our service to the Lord. We must do what we can to set things right if we want to be used of God as much as we can be.

d. **But avoid foolish and ignorant disputes**: Walking clean also means staying clear of endless disputes and arguments. These distracting interests can limit how much God can use us.

3. (24-26) The kind of attitude God can use: The gentle servant.

And a servant of the Lord must not quarrel but be gentle to all, able to teach, patient, in humility correcting those who are in opposition, if God perhaps will grant them repentance, so that they may know the truth, and *that* they may come to their senses *and escape* the snare of the devil, having been taken captive by him to *do* his will.

a. **A servant of the Lord must not quarrel but be gentle to all**: The great men of our world are not usually thought of as servants nor as gentle. Yet in the kingdom of God, greatness is marked by being **a servant of the Lord** and by being **gentle to all**.

i. "Paul's meaning is that gentleness should be shown even to those who least deserve it, and even if at first there is no apparent hope of progress, still the challenge must be accepted." (Calvin)

b. **A servant of the Lord must**: When Paul wrote to Timothy about **a servant of the Lord**, he told him about some of the basic characteristics of a godly pastor.

i. Timothy **must not quarrel but be gentle to all**. It was not his job as a pastor to pick fights and to look for conflict. Some men only feel energized and motivated if they have an argument; Timothy (and every pastor) should be of a different sort.

ii. Timothy must be **able to teach**. With the great emphasis Paul placed on God's Word, a pastor who is not **able to teach** is like a surgeon who can't use a scalpel.

iii. Timothy must be **patient**. God's work often takes time. Sometimes we can see why it takes so much time, sometimes we can't – but God is not in a hurry, and wants us to learn how to patiently trust Him.

iv. Timothy must be **in humility correcting those who are in opposition**: The gentleness and patience Timothy must have does not mean he is to never confront those who need to be confronted; but he must do it **in humility**.

c. **In humility correcting those who are in opposition**: Paul specifically told Timothy how to correct these opposing ones.

i. **If God perhaps will grant them repentance**: They need to repent, and this repentance will never happen apart from a work of God in their heart.

ii. **If God perhaps will grant them repentance**: The idea is not, "Maybe God will or maybe God won't grant them repentance." The idea is more, "It's remarkable thing to see this work of God, and I won't presume upon it happening."

iii. **So that they may know the truth, and that they may come to their senses**: Anyone who fights against God is deceived and must come to their senses; repentance flows as someone comes to the truth in this way.

iv. **And escape the snare of the devil, having been taken captive by him**: Those who are in opposition to God's work, whether they know it or not, are bound in a demonic deception, and are doing the devil's work. They need to **escape the snare of the devil**, and God is ready to set them free.

d. **Taken captive by him to do his will**: Paul spoke of those who serve the devil and those who serve God. There is a choice for every person, every Christian, who they will decide to serve.

i. To be a servant of the Lord – a vessel of honor for Him – we must be empty, clean, and available. If we refuse to empty ourselves, clean ourselves, and make ourselves available to the Lord, we will find ourselves captive to the devil in one sense or another.

2 Timothy 3 – Perilous Times and Precious Truth

"As he lies in his cell, a prisoner of the Lord, Paul is still preoccupied with the future of the gospel. His mind dwells now on the evil of the times, now on the diffidence of Timothy. Timothy is so weak, and the opposition so strong." (John Stott)

A. Perilous times mean that discernment matters.

1. (1) Perilous times in the **last days**.

But know this, that in the last days perilous times will come:

a. **In the last days perilous times will come**: The word translated **perilous** has the idea of troubles, difficulty, and stressful situations. This sort of atmosphere will mark the **last days**.

i. "The word was used in classical Greek both of dangerous wild animals and of the raging sea. Its only other New Testament occurrence is in the story of the two Gaderene demoniacs who were as savage and untamed as wild beasts and whom Matthew describes as 'so *fierce* that no one could pass that way' (Matthew 8:28)." (Stott)

ii. The characteristics Paul will describe speak not of bad *times*, but of bad *people*. "We should note what the hardness or danger of this time is in Paul's view to be, not war, not famine or diseases, nor any of the other calamities or ills that befall the body, but the wicked and depraved ways of men." (Calvin)

iii. "The description in this and in the following verses the Papists apply to the Protestants; the Protestants in turn apply it to the Papists; *Schoettgen* to the *Jews*; and others to *heretics* in general… but it is probable that the apostle had some particular age in view, in which there should appear some very essential corruption of Christianity." (Clarke)

b. **In the last days**: This is a broad term in the New Testament, broad enough to where one could say that **the last days** began with the birth of the Church on the Day of Pentecost (Acts 2:17). The days of the Messiah mark **the last days**; yet the term is especially appropriate to the season immediately before the return of Jesus and the consummation of all things.

i. Though some think that any attention paid to the **last days** or Biblical prophecy is frivolous, we should be able to discern when the **last days** are; or at least when world conditions are like the Bible described they would be in the **last days**.

ii. "There are sanguine brethren who are looking forward to everything growing better and better and better, until, at last, this present age ripens into a millennium. They will not be able to sustain their hopes, for Scripture gives them no solid basis to rest upon... Apart from the second Advent of our Lord, the world is more likely to sink into a pandemonium than to rise into a millennium." (Spurgeon)

iii. In Matthew 16:1-4, Jesus rebuked the religious leaders of His day because they did not or would not understand the meaning of their times: *Hypocrites! You know how to discern the face of the sky, but you cannot discern the signs of the times* (Matthew 16:3). It is possible that Jesus would have the same rebuke for some Christians today who are unaware of the **last days** and the soon return of Jesus Christ.

2. (2-5) A description of the human condition in the *last days*.

For men will be lovers of themselves, lovers of money, boasters, proud, blasphemers, disobedient to parents, unthankful, unholy, unloving, unforgiving, slanderers, without self-control, brutal, despisers of good, traitors, headstrong, haughty, lovers of pleasure rather than lovers of God, having a form of godliness but denying its power. And from such people turn away!

a. **Men will be lovers of themselves**: This is certainly characteristic of our present age, when men and women are encouraged to love themselves. People are told to love themselves unconditionally and that such self-love is the foundation for a healthy human personality.

i. We don't need to be encouraged to love ourselves; we naturally have such a love. Neither should we be taught to hate ourselves, but as Paul said in Romans 12:3: *For I say, through the grace given to me, to everyone who is among you, not to think of himself more highly than he ought to think, but to think soberly, as God has dealt to each one a measure of faith.* We must see ourselves as we really are – both the bad of what we are in the flesh and the glory of what we are in Jesus Christ.

ii. This love of self is the foundation for all the depravity that follows in Paul's description: "But readers should note that *lovers of themselves,* which comes first, can be regarded as the source from which all the others that follow spring." (Calvin)

iii. "It is no accident that the first of these qualities will be *a life that is centred in self*. The adjective used is *philautos*, which means *self-loving*. Love of self is the basic sin, from with all others flow. The moment a man makes his own will the centre of life, divine and human relationships are destroyed, obedience to God and charity to men both become impossible. The essence of Christianity is not the enthronement but the obliteration of self." (Barclay)

iv. "'Lovers of self' aptly heads the list since it is the essence of all sin and the root from which all the other characteristics spring. The word is literally 'self-lovers' and points to the fact that the center of gravity of the natural man is self rather than God." (Hiebert)

b. **Men will be… lovers of money**: The love of money is nothing new, but today people have the ability to pursue our love of money like never before.

i. In recent years newspapers featured a story about a woman named Brenda Blackman, who enjoyed some measure of success teaching a course titled *How to Marry Money*. The course attempts to show men and women how to marry rich, and costs $39 per person. In the course Blackman offered helpful hints, such as how to search through your prospective mate's checkbooks to study their deposits and then assess their income levels. She built her student's confidence by leading them in a chant several times through the lecture: "I want to be rich! I deserve to be rich! I am rich! I was born to be rich!" In one class, Blackman was asked by a woman if it was all right to settle for a man whose income was about $100,000 a year. "No way," she replied. What if he was perfect in every other way? "If he was in his peak earning years and he was maxed out at $100,000 – forget it," Blackman advised. When someone asked her about the place of love in such relationships, Blackman said that finding a mate with that much money is the hard part; learning to love that person is easy by comparison. "How could you not love someone who is doing all these wonderful things for you?" she said. Blackman was single as she taught these courses.

c. **Men will be… boasters, proud, blasphemers**: Boasting, pride, and blasphemy are nothing new; but today, they seem far more prominent than ever.

i. Boasting, pride, and blasphemy each act as if *I* am the most important person. Each of them say, "You don't matter and God does not matter. All that matters is me."

ii. Today boasting, pride, and blasphemy are apparent everywhere, especially among the celebrities that our cultures idolizes. Many people today become wealthy by calculated boasting, pride, and blasphemy.

d. **Men will be… disobedient to parents**: Since the mid 1960s there has been a frightening breakdown in the authority once assumed by a child towards their parents.

i. Several years ago a judge in Orlando Florida ruled that an 11-year-old boy had the right to seek a "divorce" from his parents so that he could be adopted by a foster family. But though there are few legal divorces from parents by children, it is far more common that young people simply disregard their parents.

ii. In the 1990s, a 13-year-old Los Angeles area graffiti vandal was quoted in the *Los Angeles Times*: "It's like a family to belong to a crew. They watch your back, you watch theirs. You kick it everyday with them… You get friendship, love, supplies, everything." He also says: "I'll tag anything… Now I don't care. Well, sort of. I wouldn't like no one to write on my stuff. I do it to get known, to get up, regardless if people feel that I'm causing damage to property. I'd say the damage I've done is quite a bit. During the day I carry a screwdriver or a knife for protection. But at night I carry a gun. I have three guns. I hide them. My mom took a .38 from me. I'm getting it back." When asked about once when he got caught, he said: "My parents sort of talked to me about it. Of course they told me, 'Don't do it again.' But I'm not gonna listen, and they don't have to know about it."

e. **Men will be… unthankful, unholy, unloving, unforgiving**: Ever since Adam, humankind has been marked by these things to one degree or another. Here, Paul said these things will be especially prevalent *in the last days*.

i. **Unloving** (translated *without natural affection* in the KJV) literally means, "without family love." Paul said that the end times would be marked by an attitude of growing disregard of normal family love and obligation.

f. **Men will be… slanderers**: Men have always told hurtful lies about other men; but today, in media and in politics, slander has been elevated to both big business and big money.

i. In politics, candidates routinely and knowingly distort their opponent's positions, just to make their competition look bad – and they don't feel bad at all about the lying if it helps them get elected. In media, editors and news directors serve as prosecutor, judge, jury, and executioner to innocents who are wrongly suspected – and usually refuse to apologize when they are proven to be wrong.

g. **Men will be… without self control**: The story of no self-control can be written across almost everything today – sex, drugs, alcohol, food, work. Whatever we do, we often do it out of control.

> i. In the 1990s the *Los Angeles Times* published an article about Michelle, who was a successful writer and editor. She feared the day her husband might discover her secret stash of credit cards, her secret post office box or the other tricks she used to hide how much money she spent shopping for herself. "I make as much money as my husband… If I want a $500 suit from Ann Taylor, I deserve it and don't want to be hassled about it. So the easiest thing to do is lie," she explained. Last year, when her husband forced her to destroy one of her credit cards, Michelle went out and got a new one without telling him. "I do live in fear. If he discovers this new VISA, he'll kill me." A school teacher explained more: "Men just don't understand that shopping is our drug of choice," she joked, even while admitting that some months her salary goes exclusively to paying the minimum balance on her credit cards. "Walking through the door of South Coast Plaza is like walking though the gates of heaven. God made car trunks for women to hide shopping bags in." A young professional named Mary explained: "Shopping is my recreation. It's my way of pampering myself. When you walk into [a mall] and you see all the stores, it's like something takes over and you get caught up in it."

h. **Men will be… brutal**: Cruelty and brutality are nothing new in the world; but Paul wrote by inspiration of the Holy Spirit that the *last days* would be marked by a particular brutality.

> i. A newspaper article in the 1990s described how an Oxnard man was accused of murdering his roommate after the two disagreed over the brand of beer the man had brought home. The accused man brought home Natural Light, and the murdered man wanted him to bring home Michelob. As he poured the Natural Light down the kitchen sink, he was stabbed to death.

> ii. We like to think of ourselves as more advanced than previous generations; but surely more people have been murdered in our century than ever before; these are violent, brutal times.

i. **Men will be… despisers of good**: There just seem to be too many examples of this in modern society to pick out examples. For one example, there was a time when most people thought letting people live was good and killing them was generally a bad thing. Today, we live in a culture when the simple good of *life* is now despised and attacked, through abortion, through the glorifying of violence and murder, and through euthanasia.

i. On March 6, 1996, the U.S. 9th Circuit Court of Appeals declared the United States Constitution gives every American the right to kill someone else. Essentially, the court said that if you *think* someone might want to die – even if they have never said so – you can kill them and no law can stop you. You can kill someone if you are a doctor, a nurse, a pharmacist, a family member, or a "significant other" to a person you think wants to die. From the Judge's ruling: "When patients are no longer able to pursue liberty or happiness and do not wish to pursue life," they can be killed. The Federal Judge directly tied his decision to the right to abortion on demand. The reasoning seems to be that if the state must allow us to kill humans in the womb, it must also allow them to kill them later.

j. **Men will be… traitors, headstrong, haughty, lovers of pleasure rather than lovers of God**: These characteristics are all about one thing: *Self.* Men are **traitors** because of *self,* they are **headstrong** because of *self,* they are **haughty** because of *self,* and they are **lovers of pleasure rather than lovers of God** because of *self.*

i. This attitude marks our current age. For example, think of national advertising slogans from the late 1990s:

- *Nothing is taboo.*
- *Break all the rules.*
- *To know no boundaries.*
- *Relax: No rules here.*
- *Peel off inhibitions. Find your own road.*
- *We are all hedonists and want to do what feels good. That's what makes us human.*
- *Living without boundaries.*
- *Just do it.*

The message is the same: You make your own rules. You answer to no one. You are the one that matters. Your universe revolves around you.

ii. We don't have to choose between pleasure and God. Serving God is the ultimate pleasure; Psalm 16:11 says, *At Your right hand are pleasures forevermore.* But we do have to choose between the *love* of pleasure and the *love* of God. Living for God will give you many pleasures, but they only come as you love God first and refuse to love the pleasures themselves.

k. **Having a form of godliness but denying its power**: In our self-obsessed world, people feel very free to have a "salad bar" religion – they pick and choose what they want. They feel free to be very "spiritual," but sense no obligation to be *Biblical*.

i. In the late 1990s it was reported that the Reverend John Canning delivered the eulogy after Leo and Hazel Gleese were slain, telling mourners that he had been so close to the couple that he could call them Mom and Dad. On Friday, six weeks later, Canning was led off to jail in handcuffs, charged with beating and strangling the 90-year-old couple. Police say the Gleeses were killed in their home January 2 after they discovered Canning had abused the power of attorney they gave him and was stealing their savings. "It's the most despicable thing I've ever heard of," said Phil Ramer, a Florida Department of Law Enforcement agent. "Of all people in the world you should be able to trust, it's your pastor. They couldn't do it in this case, and he wound up killing them." The pastor was a suspect from the start because he waited a day to report he found the couple dead in their home. "When it takes somebody a day to report two dead bodies, it doesn't take a rocket scientist to say who the suspect is," Ramer said. The minister passed the time before reporting the deaths by spending a day at the beach and dining out with friends.

ii. A 63-year-old married woman wrote to Dear Abby to justify her adultery. She writes: "He's also married. We meet once a week at a motel for three hours of heaven. My husband knows nothing about this, and neither does my lover's wife. Sex with my husband is even better now, and it's not as though I am denying my husband anything. I teach a class at church every week, but for some reason, I feel no guilt."

iii. When we talk about the **power** of godliness, we often mean it in the sense of "power to give me what I want." But this is exactly *opposite* of what Paul meant here. The **power** of godliness that men will despise in the last days is the power it should have to guide their lives; power in the sense of rightful authority – and many, many, today deny that God has the *power* to tell them what to do through His Word.

l. **From such people turn away!** The command to **turn away** from people described by the characteristics in this list is especially difficult in our present day.

i. People who do the things on this list are not only common today but hey are often also our cultural heroes. The simple responsibility of Christians is to **turn away** not only these attitudes, but also from the people who do these things.

ii. Many think it is enough if they themselves are not like this, and give little heed to the company they keep. But if we spend time with people like this – either personally or by allowing us to entertain us – they will influence on us. As Paul wrote in 1 Corinthians 15:33: *Do not be deceived: "Evil company corrupts good habits."*

iii. **From such turn away** also means that Paul knew those marked by the spirit of the last days were present in Timothy's own day. However, we should expect that they would be even more numerous and have increased power in the last days shortly before the return of Jesus.

iv. "This exhortation clearly implies that Paul did not consider the state of moral depravity just pictured as wholly a matter of the future. He was keenly aware that the evils about which he was forewarning were already at work." (Hiebert)

3. (6-7) The strategy of the corrupt in the last days.

For of this sort are those who creep into households and make captives of gullible women loaded down with sins, led away by various lusts, always learning and never able to come to the knowledge of the truth.

a. **Those who creep into households**: Paul knew that they dangers were in the world in his day and would be increasingly present in the last days before the return of Jesus. However, he seemed especially concerned that these would **creep into households**. It is one thing to have such evil present in the world; it is another thing to allow it into your home.

b. **Make captives of gullible women**: Those marked by the last days depravity Paul mentioned in the previous verses want to take others captive, and it can do this among the **gullible**, those who will believe or pay attention to most anything if it is packaged the right way.

i. One should know if they are indeed one of these **captives** that Paul mentioned, bound by the influence of this end times rejection of God and celebration of self. There is one effective way to know: walk away from any kind of worldly influence and see if there are chains that make your escape difficult. Take a week off from letting *anything* marked by the spirit of the last days into your household – and see if chains bind you back to those things.

ii. Paul singled out **gullible women** simply because in that day, women spent far more time at home than the men, and were far more exposed to any corruption that would infiltrate the household. "Also he speaks here of women rather than men, for they are more liable to be taken in by such impostors." (Calvin)

c. **Led away by various lusts**: Obviously, the spirit of the last days finds its appeal to us by exciting **various lusts** within us. It appeals to the desire to be excited sexually, or romantically, or to have our desires for comfort or wealth or status satisfied.

d. **Always learning and never able to come to the knowledge of the truth**: The spirit of the last days has a certain intelligence about it; the high priests of the spirit of the last days know how to make things work and how to lead us **away by various lusts**. But for all their skill, for all of their marketing brilliance and knowledge, they never come to **truth**.

> i. Indeed, the spirit of the last days has a problem with the idea of "true truth" altogether, because it believes that we each are the center of our own universe and we each create our own truth. According to the spirit of the last days there is no truth outside of ourselves, so we can learn and learn and learn, but we will never come to God's eternal truth.

> ii. "There are many professors of Christianity still who answer the above description. They hear, repeatedly hear, it may be, good sermons; but, as they seldom meditate on what they hear, they derive little profit from the ordinances of God. They have no more grace *now* than they had *several years ago*, though hearing all the while, and perhaps not wickedly departing from the Lord. They do not meditate, they do not think, they do not reduce what they hear to practice; therefore, even under the preaching of an apostle, they could not become wise to salvation." (Clarke)

4. (8-9) An example of this sort of corrupt human condition: **Jannes and Jambres**, who **resisted Moses**.

Now as Jannes and Jambres resisted Moses, so do these also resist the truth: men of corrupt minds, disapproved concerning the faith; but they will progress no further, for their folly will be manifest to all, as theirs also was.

a. **Jannes and Jambres**: Though they were not named for us in the Exodus account, these two men are the Egyptian magicians who opposed Moses before Pharaoh (Exodus 7:8-13, 7:19-23, 8:5-7, and 8:16-19).

b. **Jannes and Jambres resisted Moses**: These were able to work *real miracles* – not mere parlor tricks – but by the power of darkness and not the power of God. When Moses cast down his rod and it turned into a serpent, Jannes and Jambres could do the same. When he turned water into blood, they could do the same. When Moses brought forth a plague of frogs, Jannes and Jambres could do the same. Yet eventually they could not match God miracle-for-miracle, and their occult powers were shown to be inferior to God's power.

i. The ability to do miracles by the power of darkness and the willingness to receive them as authentic will characterize the end times (Revelation 13:13-15 and 2 Thessalonians 2:9).

ii. Some of us are amazed by any spiritual power that is *real*, without carefully thinking that real power may have a demonic source instead of a Godly source. And even if a psychic or new age power seems to feel right, we must not be seduced by it because demonic powers can come masquerading as *angels of light* (2 Corinthians 11:15).

c. **Resisted Moses**: The resistance of truth by Jannes and Jambres was shown by their ability to cooperate with demonic powers to do miracles. In the last days, men will also **resist** the truth.

d. **They will progress no further**: Even as **Jannes and Jambres** were eventually put to shame (though for a while they matched Moses "miracle for miracle") and were eventually compelled to give reluctant glory to God, so also will the evil men of the last days. Even as Jannes and Jambres' power had limits, so does Satan's power, even in the last days – God is still in control.

i. This is the message of great hope in the midst of this great darkness – the spirit of the last days has an answer to it in Jesus Christ. The spirit of the last days is not stronger than the power of Jesus. The glorious truth is that we don't have to be bound by the spirit of our times; we don't have to be slaves to self and have our universe revolve around something as puny as our selves. There is hope, triumphant hope, in Jesus.

ii. "What is remarkable about this analogy, however, is not just that the Asian false teachers are likened to the Egyptian magicians but that Paul is thereby likening himself to Moses!" (Stott)

B. Faithfulness to God in difficulty and opposition.

1. (10-12) Persecution and following Jesus.

But you have carefully followed my doctrine, manner of life, purpose, faith, longsuffering, love, perseverance, persecutions, afflictions, which happened to me at Antioch, at Iconium, at Lystra—what persecutions I endured. And out of *them* all the Lord delivered me. Yes, and all who desire to live godly in Christ Jesus will suffer persecution.

a. **But you**: Paul has just described the kind of people that will threaten the earth in the last days and which Timothy must contend with in his own day. **But you** showed that Paul drew a clear dividing line between Timothy and those ruled by the spirit of the last days.

b. **You have carefully followed**: This is what made Timothy from the spirit of his age. He had **carefully followed** Paul's **doctrine, manner of life, purpose, faith, longsuffering, love, perseverance, persecutions, afflictions**.

 i. **Carefully followed** means that Paul did not merely *teach* Timothy these things in an academic sense; Timothy learned these things by **carefully following** Paul's example. The best kind of Christianity is not only *taught*, it is also *caught* by seeing it lived out in other people.

 ii. It all began with Timothy catching Paul's **doctrine**. The reason Paul lived the way he lived was because he believed certain things. What we believe will determine how we live.

 iii. Timothy caught Paul's **manner of life**: There was just a certain way that Paul lived, and Timothy was around him enough to learn it and follow it.

 iv. Timothy caught Paul's **purpose**: Paul's life had a purpose. It was not without direction. He was going somewhere, and that purpose had been established by God. Timothy saw that in Paul, he caught it, and he wanted to live his life that way.

 v. Timothy caught Paul's **faith, longsuffering**, and **love**: you could see in Paul that he had a **faith** not everyone had, and Timothy wanted to catch it. Paul was **longsuffering** – that is, patient with the little irritations of people and life in a special way, and he had a **love** that made him stand out. Remember all of these flowed forth from the **doctrine** – the truth – Paul held on to and Timothy carefully followed.

c. **Perseverance, persecutions, afflictions**: Timothy also caught these from Paul. We might think that the person who lives their life with the right **doctrine**, with the right **manner of life, purpose, faith, longsuffering**, and **love** would be loved and accepted by everyone – but they are not.

 i. In fact, some level of persecution is *certain* for people who carefully follow this kind of life: **Yes, and all who desire to live godly in Christ Jesus will suffer persecution.**

 ii. In our own day, Christians are being persecuted all over the world – in China, in the Muslim world, even in Russia, where a strong anti-missionary law was just passed. And we can face persecution in a social way today.

iii. Christians are persecuted for the same reason Jesus was persecuted: *And this is the condemnation, that the light has come into the world, and men loved darkness rather than light, because their deeds were evil.* (John 3:19)

d. **Which happened to me at Antioch, at Iconium, at Lystra**: Paul reminded Timothy of the specific occasions of persecution which he endured.

- **At Antioch**, where Paul was kicked out of the city for preaching the gospel (Acts 13:50).

- **At Iconium**, where Paul was almost executed by stoning (Acts 14:5).

- **At Lystra**, where they actually did stone Paul and leave him for dead (Acts 14:19).

e. **And out of them all the Lord delivered me**: Paul remembered this as he sat in prison and waited for execution. He knew that God was completely able to deliver him again, or that He might not. Paul seemed at complete peace, leaving it in the Lord's hands. Persecution was not going to stop Paul from following hard after Jesus Christ.

i. Persecution must not stop Christians today. We may not face much violent or even economic persecution in our culture; but there is a great deal of social persecution Christians must deal with. 1 Peter 4:4 describes the mind-set of many of those who socially persecute Christians: *They think it strange that you do not run with them in the same flood of dissipation, speaking evil of you.* Does anyone think you are strange?

ii. If we are not willing to have others think us strange; if we are not willing to be rejected by some for the sake of Jesus Christ; if we are not willing to be an outcast before some people, then we can never be true followers of Jesus Christ.

2. (13-15) The course of evil men and the course of the godly.

But evil men and impostors will grow worse and worse, deceiving and being deceived. But you must continue in the things which you have learned and been assured of, knowing from whom you have learned *them,* **and that from childhood you have known the Holy Scriptures, which are able to make you wise for salvation through faith which is in Christ Jesus.**

a. **But evil men and impostors will grow worse and worse**: **Evil men** refers to the obvious, open enemies of Jesus; **impostors** refers to those who appear good and many think of as fine, but they are actually destructive forces among Jesus' followers.

i. These two kinds of people (**evil men** and **impostors**) will **grow worse and worse, deceiving and being deceived**. Paul gave us insight into how many people are effective deceivers among God's people – they themselves are **being deceived**.

ii. Motives are important, but we can sometimes place too much importance on them. Much harm has been done by people who were sincerely deceived and who tried to do wrong things out of wonderful motives – and because others look at their wonderful hearts, they accept their dangerous deceptions. We can't always go only by motives in others; we must measure them also by the *truth*.

b. **But you must continue in the things which you have learned**: This is the key point to this section, around which the rest of the section develops. The command itself is simple enough to understand. He told Timothy to abide – it's the same ancient Greek verb as when John wrote, *therefore let that abide in you which you heard from the beginning* (1 John 2:20).

i. It was as if Paul wrote this: "Timothy, you learned these things. Right now you firmly believe them. Now, you have to **continue in the things which you have learned**. The important thing is to abide in them, to continue in them, to never let them go."

ii. **But you**: A.T. Robertson called this an "Emphatic contrast." Timothy was to strongly set himself *against* the course that some other men took.

iii. Yet the words "**But you**" go back even further, marking a contrast to what came earlier in the letter.

- There are approved and disapproved workers – **you must continue** in the things which you have learned.

- There will be dangerous times and dangerous men in the last days – **you must continue** in the things which you have learned.

- There will be hardship and sometimes persecution as you follow the Lord – but **you must continue** in the things which you have learned.

c. **You must continue in the things which you have learned**: The plural suggests that the command is somewhat broader. The core is faithfulness to God's word, but through the letter we see that this refers to a pattern of ministry.

i. This was all centered on God's word, but "**the things which you have learned**" seems to be more than just Paul's Bible studies; it was those, but also his pattern of ministry.

ii. This pattern of ministry doesn't deal much with specifics, such as when to have Christian services, how long to have them, a schedule for what to do during service, and so on. The emphasis is on a pattern, a philosophy, and then Timothy was to implement that into his own situation.

d. **You must continue in the things which you have learned**: The rest of the passage – up until the fourth chapter – simply describes for us what this means, and why it was so important for Timothy to do this.

i. It is wonderful to see that God gives us *reasons* to continue – it isn't just, "Well, that is what we do" or "We have always done it that way." God is good enough to give us *reasons*.

e. **And been assured of**: This puts the idea in the past tense, as if this was something that Timothy was once assured of, but perhaps now he wasn't so sure. Perhaps he wavered from time to time, so Paul called him back to this.

f. **Knowing from whom you have learned them**: Continue in the things you have learned, *remembering who taught you those things*. It was as if Paul wrote, "Remember, Timothy: you learned these things *from me*." Paul was too humble to say his own name here, but it certainly seems that is what he meant.

i. There is some debate among manuscripts whether **whom** is singular or plural. I think the context pushes us towards the idea that it is singular; Paul here refers to his own influence on Timothy.

- Paul led him to Christ.
- Paul gave him ministry opportunity
- Paul taught him by both word and example.
- Paul laid hands on him in ordination.
- Paul guided and mentored him in the midst of ministry.

ii. So, Timothy was to remember who taught him these things, **knowing from whom you have learned them**. Paul's idea included:

- Remember how I strongly and confidently I believe these things.
- Remember the love with which I believe these things.
- Remember the urgency with which I believe these things.

g. **That from childhood you have known the Holy Scriptures**: Continue in the things you have learned, *that you have received as a heritage*. This truth didn't begin with Timothy or even with Paul, but it is part of a long heritage that was passed on to Timothy.

i. **From childhood** means that it came to him through the influence of his grandmother and mother – Lois and Eunice, respectively. From his young childhood, they taught him.

ii. Timothy learned this starting in **childhood**. "The story of Mistress Elizabeth Wheatenhall, daughter of Mr. Anthony Wheatenhall, of Tenterden in Kent, late deceased, is very memorable. She being brought up by her aunt, the Lady Wheatenhall, before she was nine years old (not much above eight), could say all the New Testament by heart; yea, being asked where any words thereof were, she could presently name book, chapter, and verse." (Trapp)

iii. **Holy Scriptures**: This use here referred to the Old Testament, because that is what Timothy would have learned from his grandmother Eunice and his mother Lois.

iv. **From childhood you have known**: Timothy had known the word of God from his earliest years; yet see how strong the exhortation is from Paul that he *continue* in them! Nothing is assumed; the furthest thing from Paul's mind is an attitude that says, "Well of course we are all founded on the Bible and we can assume that and move on to other things." For Paul this was never assumed – not even with his trusted protégé Timothy.

h. **From childhood you have known the Holy Scriptures**: It's as if Paul said this: "Timothy, continue in what you received from me. But never forget that it didn't start with me; it's a heritage that was passed on to you. You came into contact with all this long before you ever knew me. You came into contact with this heritage through **the Holy Scriptures**."

i. We're happy to belong to the same church as Moody and Spurgeon, and Luther and Zwingli; the same church as Wesley and Whitefield, and Polycarp and Ignatius. We are part of them and they are part of us, because we are connected by our trust in the same Jesus, revealed to us by the same **Holy Scriptures**.

i. **Which are able to make you wise for salvation through faith which is in Christ Jesus**: Continue in the things you have learned, *because of their great value*. There is no wisdom greater than this in the world. Your wisdom about 20 other subjects means nothing if you are not **wise for salvation**.

i. This is something each generation must acquire for itself and then hold on to – the appreciation for the wisdom of the Bible, and a deliberate forsaking of any human wisdom that opposes or replaces what the Bible teaches.

ii. We don't think for a moment that mere Bible knowledge saves; there are those who know the words of the Bible well yet are not **wise for salvation**. Yet those words mixed with **faith** do make one wise for salvation.

3. (16-17) Timothy must continue with confidence in the Holy Scriptures.

All Scripture *is* given by inspiration of God, and *is* profitable for doctrine, for reproof, for correction, for instruction in righteousness, that the man of God may be complete, thoroughly equipped for every good work.

a. **All Scripture**: This indicates *more* than the Hebrew Scriptures. If Paul meant the exact same thing here as what Timothy learned as a child, he might have said "Those Scriptures" referring back to verse 15, or he might have just repeated the exact phrase, "**Holy Scriptures**."

i. Paul changed his wording here because he recognized that what God uniquely brought forth from the apostles and prophets in his time was also **Scripture**; it was also the God-breathed word of God. This included what he and others knew was emerging as the written form of the *foundation of the apostles and prophets* mentioned in Ephesians 2:20.

ii. This would fulfill the promise Jesus made that the Holy Spirit would speak to the apostles and lead them into all truth.

iii. There is no doubt that Paul thought this way – knowing that God was bringing forth a New Testament through the apostles and prophets of the first century.

- Paul commanded the public congregational reading of his letters, *as would be done with the Hebrew Scriptures* (Colossians 4:16, 1 Thessalonians 5:27).

- Paul called his own message *the word of God* (1 Thessalonians 2:13).

- In 1 Timothy 5:18, Paul combined a quotation from the Old Testament, and some words of Jesus recorded in Luke 10:7 and he called *both* of them "Scripture."

iv. Paul wasn't the only one who thought this way. 2 Peter 3:15b-16 indicates the same idea, especially when Peter included Paul's writings under the heading, *Scriptures*.

v. All this reminds us that even in Apostolic times, they were well aware that God was bringing forth more **Holy Scripture**, just as Jesus promised, just as Paul described, just as Peter understood.

b. **All Scripture is given by inspiration of God**: Paul exhorted Timothy, "Continue in these things *because the Bible comes from God and not man. It is a God-inspired book, breathed out from God Himself.*"

i. This means something more than saying that God inspired the men who wrote it, though we believe that He did; God also inspired the very words they wrote. We notice it doesn't say, "All Scripture writers are inspired by God," even though that was true. Yet it doesn't go far enough. *The words they wrote were breathed by God.*

ii. It isn't that God breathed into the human authors. That is true, but not what Paul says here. He says that God breathed out of them His Holy Word.

iii. Some protest: "This statement doesn't mean anything because it is self-referential. Anyone could write a book and say that it is inspired by God." *Of course* it is self-referential. *Of course* the Bible says it is Holy Scripture. If it did not make that claim, critics would attack the lack of such a claim saying, "The Bible itself claims no inspiration."

iv. Yet the difference is that the Bible's claim to be Holy Scripture has been tested and proven through the centuries. Every generation gives rise to those who really believe they will put the last nails in the coffin that will bury the Bible – yet it never, never works. The Bible outlives and outworks and out-influences all of its critics. It is an anvil that has worn out many, many hammers.

v. And to the critic who claims, "Anyone could write a book and say that it is inspired by God" we simply say, *please do*. Write your book, give it every claim of inspiration, and let's see how it compares to the Bible in any way you want to compare. We invite the smarter critics of the Bible to give us another Bible, something more inspired, something with more life-changing power. The great critic or professor or skeptic is surely smarter than a Galilean fisherman 2,000 years ago, having all the qualifications, all the culture, all the brainpower necessary. It should be *easy* for them to write something greater than the Bible.

vi. But of course this is impossible; there is no equal to the Bible and there never will be. The grass withers, the flower fades, but the word of our Lord stands forever. What can compare to the Bible? What is the chaff to the wheat?

- There is no book like it in its *continuity and consistency*.

- There is no book like it in its honesty.

- There is no book like it in its circulation.

- There is no book like it in its survival.

- There is no book like it in its influence and life-changing power.

c. **By inspiration of God**: One may easily argue that the Bible is a *unique* book, but it does not prove that God inspired it. For greater evidence, one can look to the phenomenon of fulfilled prophecy.

i. Peter wrote about how we can know the Scriptures are really from God and he spoke about his own certainty because he saw Jesus miraculously transfigured before his own eyes and he heard a voice from heaven say, *This is my beloved Son, in whom I am well pleased.* Yet, Peter said that we even have something *more* certain than a voice from heaven in knowing the Bible is from God: *We also have the prophetic word made more sure, which you do well to heed as a light that shines in a dark place* (2 Peter 1:19).

ii. God's ability to precisely predict future events in the Bible is His own way of building proof for the Bible right into the text. It proves that it was authored by Someone who not only can see the future, but Who can also shape the future.

iii. For example, there are at least 332 distinct Old Testament predictions regarding the Messiah which Jesus fulfilled perfectly (such as His birth in Bethlehem, His emergence from Egypt, His healing of the sick, His death on the cross, and so forth). Collectively, the combination of this evidence together is absolutely overwhelming.

iv. Professor Peter Stoner has calculated that the probability of any one man fulfilling eight of these prophesies is one in 100,000,000,000,000,000 (10 to the 17th power); that many silver dollars would cover the state of Texas two feet deep. Stoner says that if you consider 48 of the prophecies, the odds become one in 10 to the 157th power.

d. **All Scripture is given by inspiration of God**: Remember that one may believe in the inspiration of the Bible in *principle*, but deny it in *practice*.

- We do this by imposing our own meaning on the text instead of letting it speak for itself.

- We do this by putting more of our self in the message than what God says.

- We do this by being more interested in our opinions when we preach than in explaining and proclaiming what God has said.

- We do this by lazy study and sloppy exposition.

- Instead, we honor God and His word by, as much as possible, simply letting the text explain and teach itself; to speak for itself.

  i. "False doctrine cannot prevail long where the sacred Scriptures are read and studied. Error prevails only where the book of God is withheld from the people. The religion that fears the Bible is not the religion of God." (Clarke)

  ii. In 2005 the *London Times* reported that a new "teaching document" issued by the Roman Catholic bishops of England, Wales and Scotland warns that Catholics should not take the Bible literally -- that it's not infallible. "We should not expect to find in Scripture full scientific accuracy or complete historical precision," they say in the booklet, *The Gift of Scripture*. So what sorts of things aren't accurate? Creation, for one. Genesis, they note, has two different, and sometimes conflicting, creation stories and cannot be considered "historical." Rather, the bishops say, it simply contains "historical traces."

e. **All Scripture**: This tells us *how much* of the Bible is inspired by God. The great Greek scholar Dean Alford understood this as meaning, "Every part of Scripture."

  i. Some try to twist this – they try to make it say, "All Scripture that <u>is</u> inspired by God is profitable" and so on. In doing this, they put themselves in the place of highest authority, because they then will tell us what is inspired and what isn't.

  ii. They claim that the grammar is elastic enough in this statement to give the translation, "All Scripture *that is* inspired by God is profitable." But this is dishonest to the text, and ignores a critical word present both in the English translation and the ancient Greek: the word **and**.

  iii. The position of **and** in the text makes it clear that Paul is asserting two truths about Scripture: that it is *both* God-breathed **and** profitable; *not* that only the God-breathed parts *are* profitable.

  iv. So we believe it forever: it is **all** inspired, *and* **all** profitable. Since it comes from a perfect God, it is perfect and without error in the original autographs; and what we have before us are extraordinarily good copies of what was originally written.

v. The reliability of our copies of what was originally written is a matter which can be decided by science and research, and though some errors have been made in copying the Scriptures through the centuries, today we have a New Testament where not more than one-one thousandth of the text is in question – and not *one* significant doctrine is in question. The numbers for the Old Testament are even more impressive.

vi. There is something else we can say about the Bible: *It is true.* And though the Bible is *not* a science text-book, when it does speak on matters of science as science (not in figures of speech or poetic hyperbole), it is *true*.

f. **And is profitable**: Paul exhorted, "Timothy, continue in these things *because the Bible is profitable*, and profitable in many ways."

i. Profitable for **doctrine**: telling us what is true about God, man, the world we live in, and the world to come.

ii. Profitable for **reproof and correction**: with the authority to rebuke us and correct us. We are all under the authority of God's word, and when the Bible exposes our doctrine or our conduct as wrong, *we are wrong*.

iii. Profitable for **instruction in righteousness**: it tells us how to live in *true* righteousness. There is perhaps here a hint of grace, because Paul knew what true righteousness was instead of the legalistic false righteousness that he depended on before his conversion.

iv. This all means something else very simple: *We can understand the Bible*. If the Bible could not be understood, there would be nothing **profitable** about it.

v. It is **profitable** when we understand it *literally*. But when we take the Bible literally, we also understand that it means that we take it as true according to its literary context. When the Bible speaks as poetry, it will use figures of speech that may not be literally true. One example is when David said, *All night I make my bed swim; I drench my couch with my tears* in Psalm 6:6. Obviously, he spoke in poetic metaphor and he did not actually float his bed with tears. But when the Bible speaks as history, it *is* historically true, when it speaks in prophecy, it *is* prophetically true.

g. **That the man of God may be complete, thoroughly equipped for every good work**: Paul exhorted, "Timothy, continue in these things *because the Bible makes you complete and thoroughly equipped for every good work*."

i. **Complete** doesn't mean that the whole Christian life is about reading the Bible, or that the only important thing in good ministry is good Bible teaching.

ii. **Complete** means the Bible leads me into everything I need. If I will be both a hearer and a doer of the word, I will be **complete** as a Christian, **thoroughly equipped for every good work.** This reminds us that we are not in the business of building sermon appreciation societies, but in equipping the saints for the work of ministry.

iii. So, I don't ignore prayer, or worship, or evangelism, or good works to a needy world – *because the Bible itself tells me to do such things.* If I will be both a hearer and a doer of the word, I will be **complete**.

h. **That the man of God may be complete**: When we come to the Bible and let God speak to us, it changes us – it makes us **complete** and transforms us.

i. One way the Bible transforms us is through our understanding. Romans 12:2 says, *do not be conformed to this world, but be transformed by the renewing of your mind, that you may prove what is that good and acceptable and perfect will of God.* When we let the Bible guide our thinking, our minds are renewed and transformed, so we begin to actually think like God thinks.

ii. But there is another level by which the Bible transforms us: by a spiritual work, a spiritual blessing which God works in us as we come to the Bible and let Him speak to us. This is a spiritual work that goes beyond our intellectual understanding. With great spiritual power beyond our intellect:

- The Bible gives us eternal life (1 Peter 1:23).
- The Bible spiritually cleanses us (Ephesians 5:26).
- The Bible gives us power against demonic spirits (Ephesians 6:17).
- The Bible brings spiritual power to heal our bodies (Matthew 8:16).
- The Bible brings us spiritual strength (Psalm 119:28).
- The Bible has the power to spiritually build faith in us (Romans 10:17).

iii. Because of this spiritual level on which the Word of God operates, we don't have to understand it all to have it be effectively working in our lives. Many people get discouraged because they feel they don't get much when they read the Bible on their own and so they give up.

We must work to understand the Bible the best we can, and read it thoughtfully and carefully, but it benefits us *spiritually* even when we don't understand it all *intellectually*.

iv. A critic once wrote a letter to a magazine saying, "Over the years, I suppose I've gone to church more than 1,000 times, and I can't remember the specific content of even one sermon over those many years. What good was it to go to church 1,000 times?" The next week, someone wrote back: "Over the past many years, I have eaten more than 1,000 meals prepared by my wife. I cannot remember the specific menu of any of those meals. But they nourished me along the way, and without them, I would be a much different man!" The Bible will do its spiritual work in us, if we will let it.

v. Paul began the chapter warning Timothy about dangerous times. Some Christians are swept away by these perilous times and some others go into hiding. Neither option is right for us. We are to stand strong and stay on the Word of God.

2 Timothy 4 – Paul's Final Testimony to Timothy

A. Paul's final testimony to Timothy.

1. (1) A solemn charge to Timothy.

I charge *you* therefore before God and the Lord Jesus Christ, who will judge the living and the dead at His appearing and His kingdom.

a. **I charge you therefore**: **Charge** translates a strong word from Biblical Greek (*diamarturomai*), also often translated *testified* (such as in Acts 8:25). The idea is that Paul gave a solemn testimony to Timothy, testimony that Timothy must heed if he would be a godly pastor.

i. "The verb *diamartyromai* has legal connections and can mean 'testify under oath' in a court of law, or to 'adjure' a witness to do so." (Stott)

b. **Before God and the Lord Jesus Christ, who will judge the living and the dead**: Paul here described the members of the court where Paul gave his testimony, thereby making it more important.

i. As Paul sat in his cold, damp prison cell, he understood there was a spiritual reality present that went beyond the walls of his cell. Spiritually, through this letter, he gave solemn testimony to his young friend and associate and he did it in the presence of the God who will judge us all.

c. **At His appearing and His kingdom**: Paul still believed in the Second Coming of Jesus Christ. He had been in ministry for more than 30 years and his earliest letters (such as 1 and 2 Thessalonians) mentioned the return of Jesus. Now, so many years and experiences later, he still believed it with all his heart.

i. "The words 'shall judge' more literally are 'is about to be judging'; they point to the fact that Paul was living in the hope of the imminent return of Christ." (Hiebert)

2. (2) The testimony: **Preach the word!**

Preach the word! Be ready in season *and* out of season. Convince, rebuke, exhort, with all longsuffering and teaching.

a. **Preach the word!** Paul's emphasis on the word of God has been constant. There are some 36 references to the true gospel in this letter and some 17 references to false teachings.

i. This constant emphasis makes Paul's point clear to Timothy:

* *Do not be ashamed of the testimony of our Lord* (2 Timothy 1:8).

* *Hold fast the pattern of sound words* (2 Timothy 1:13).

* *The things that you have heard from me among many witnesses, commit these to faithful men* (2 Timothy 2:2).

* *Rightly dividing the word of truth* (2 Timothy 2:15).

* *A servant of the Lord must be ... able to teach* (2 Timothy 2:24).

* *All Scripture is given by inspiration of God* (2 Timothy 3:16).

b. **Preach the word!** As a pastor, Timothy was not required to merely *know* the word or *like* the word or *approve* of the word; he was required to **preach the word**. The word of God must be *preached* by Timothy; it was to be the content of his message.

i. Not everyone who opens a Bible and starts talking is preaching the word. Many well-intentioned preachers are actually preaching *themselves* instead of the word. If the *focus* is on the funny stories or the touching life experiences of the preacher, he may be preaching himself.

c. **Be ready in season and out of season**: This tells us *when* the pastor should be ready to preach the word. He should be ready *always*. He should preach it when it is easy and preach it when it is hard. He should preach it when the fruit is evident and preach it when the fruit seems invisible. He should just preach it.

i. There was once a Church of England clergyman who was gloriously saved. When Jesus changed his life he started preaching the gospel to his whole parish and they all got saved. Then he started preaching in neighboring parishes, and the clergymen of those parishes were offended. They asked the bishop to make the man stop. When the bishop confronted him he said, "I hear you are always preaching and you don't seem to be doing anything else." The changed man answered, "Well bishop, I only preach during two seasons of the year." The bishop said, "I'm glad to know that; what seasons are they?" He replied, "In season and out of season!"

d. **Convince, rebuke, exhort, with all longsuffering and teaching**: In his preaching Timothy was to bring the Word of God to bear on the lives of his people. He was not to treat the word as if it were filled with interesting ideas or fascinating theories. He was to hold up the Word of God against the lives of his people and let God do His work.

3. (3-4) The need for the true preaching of the word.

For the time will come when they will not endure sound doctrine, but according to their own desires, *because* they have itching ears, they will heap up for themselves teachers; and they will turn *their* ears away from the truth, and be turned aside to fables.

a. **They will not endure sound doctrine**: Timothy needed to keep focused on the Word of God because man, by his natural instinct, does not *want* God's revelation. He would rather hear what he wants to hear – something to scratch his **itching ears**.

i. Clarke on **itching ears**: "Endless curiosity, an insatiable desire of *variety*; and they get their ears tickled with the *language* and *accent* of the person, abandoning the *good* and *faithful preacher* for the *fine speaker*."

ii. This also shows that if we *do* want to hear God's word, God is doing something wonderful in us. Left to ourselves, we would rather do it our way, but God changes our heart in wonderful ways, giving us a desire for His word.

b. **They will heap up for themselves teachers**: This reminds us that the most popular teachers are not necessarily the most faithful teachers. We shouldn't assume a teacher is scratching itching ears just because he is popular, but neither should we assume that he is faithful to God's Word just because he is popular.

c. **And be turned aside to fables**: Once people leave the Word of God they often then embrace fantastic fantasies. When a man rejects God's truth, it isn't that he believes in nothing; he will believe in *anything*.

i. To believe that the universe came about by chance is to believe a fable. This description of the evolution of the universe in a *Los Angeles Times* article is an example of one of these **fables**:

In the beginning, there was light – but also quarks and electrons. The Big Bang spewed out energy that condensed into radiation and particles. The quarks joined into protons and careened wildly about in a hot, dense, glowing goop as opaque as a star.

Time (300,000 years or so) passed. Space expanded. Matter cooled. The electrons and protons, electrically irresistible to each other, merged into neutral hydrogen, and from this marriage, the first atoms were born. Space between atoms became as transparent as crystal – pretty much the way it looks today.

The rest, as they say, is history. Atoms merged to form dust clouds, which grew into stars and galaxies and clusters. Stars used up their nuclear fuel, collapsed and exploded in recurring cycles, fusing elements in the process.

Occasionally, a stable planet condensed around a second-generations star, where carbon-based life forms grew into, among other things, cosmologists, the better to contemplate it all. (From a sidebar to a science article in the *Los Angeles Times*, titled "The Big Bang and What Followed It")

ii. It is possible for many churchgoers to turn aside from the truth and to believe many fables:

- The fable that you must *earn* your way before God.

- The fable that God only loves you when you are good.

- The fable that you should walk around thinking of yourself as better than others because you are a Christian.

4. (5) The testimony restated: **Fulfill your ministry**.

But you be watchful in all things, endure afflictions, do the work of an evangelist, fulfill your ministry.

a. **But you**: This is a word of contrast against the people mentioned in the previous sentence. Though others turned aside to fables, Timothy was to be even more dedicated to doing what God wanted him to do. Their presence was to make him more dedicated, not more discouraged.

i. "The more determined men become to despise the teachings of Christ, the more zealous should godly ministers be to assert it and the more strenuous their efforts to preserve it entire." (Calvin)

b. **Be watchful in all things**: Timothy could not fulfill his ministry unless he kept careful attention, being **watchful in all things**. Every good shepherd has his eyes open.

c. **Endure afflictions**: Ministry is just like life – there are **afflictions** to be borne with. For some this is a disturbing thought because they thought that the ministry would be one beautiful spiritual experience after another. There are plenty of wonderful blessings in serving God but there are also **afflictions** to be endured.

d. **Do the work of an evangelist**: This implies that Timothy was not particularly gifted as an evangelist but he still had to faithfully do that **work** as a preacher of God's Word.

e. **Fulfill your ministry**: Paul gave a similar command to Archippus (Colossians 4:17), and he knew what it was to fulfill his own ministry in some sense (Acts 12:25).

> i. There may be many reasons why someone's ministry goes unfulfilled and each must be earnestly battled:

> - Fear.

> - Unbelief.

> - The cares of the world.

> - The fear of man.

> - Criticism and discouragement.

> - Besetting sin.

B. The final words from Paul: his triumphant confidence.

1. (6-7) Paul's triumphant confidence.

For I am already being poured out as a drink offering, and the time of my departure is at hand. I have fought the good fight, I have finished the race, I have kept the faith.

a. **I am already being poured out as a drink offering**: A drink offering brought wine before the Lord and poured it out at His altar. It was a way to give wine to God as a sacrifice, just as an animal might be given as a sacrifice.

> i. The idea of a **drink offering** is first presented in Genesis 35:14, where Jacob poured out a drink offering before the Lord as a sacrifice. In the Mosaic Law, drink offerings could be a part of sacrifice to the Lord (Exodus 29:40-41 and Leviticus 23:13).

> ii. There was also a Roman idea here. Every Roman meal ended with a small sacrificial ritual to the gods – a cup of wine was taken and poured out before the gods. In this sense Paul said "The day is done, the meal is just about over, and I'm being poured out unto God."

> iii. **Poured out** has the idea of a *complete* giving, with no reservation. The liquid is completely emptied from the cup, and totally given to God.

> iv. So Paul was **already being poured out**. His head was not on the executioner's block yet, but his heart was there. He was *ready* to make the ultimate sacrifice. "He considers himself as on the eve of being

sacrificed, and looks upon his blood as the libation which was poured on the sacrificial offering. He could not have spoken thus positively had not the sentence of death been already passed upon him." (Clarke)

b. **The time of my departure is at hand**: Paul felt that he was in the airport and his flight to heaven was ready to depart. He waited for his boarding call.

i. Paul's exhortation to Timothy is therefore even more meaningful because he knew he was passing from the scene and Timothy must carry the torch. God's workmen pass on, but God's work continues.

c. **I have finished the race**: Throughout his ministry Paul used the picture of the race and the Christian being an athlete running that race (Philippians 3:12-14, Acts 20:24, 1 Corinthians 9:24, Hebrews 12:1). Now he knew his race was just about **finished**.

2. (8) Paul's crown of righteousness.

Finally, there is laid up for me the crown of righteousness, which the Lord, the righteous Judge, will give to me on that Day, and not to me only but also to all who have loved His appearing.

a. **There is laid up for me**: Paul knew there was a crown waiting for him in heaven, and he was ready to receive it. He was certain of it.

i. There are two main words for **crown** in the New Testament. One refers to a royal crown and the other to the victor's crown (the *stephanos*). Here Paul referred to the victor's crown – the crown that was essentially a trophy, recognizing that one had competed according to the rules and had won the victory.

ii. Before Paul was a Christian he supervised the execution of the first martyr and then began to kill as many other Christians as he could. But now at the end of his life he was ready to receive a crown – a *stephanos*. It is likely that he remembered the name of the first martyr, who died at Paul's own hands: *Stephanos* (Stephen).

iii. In that day winners in the world of sports received a crown of olive or ivy leaves that soon withered and died. But the crown for God's people lasts forever (1 Corinthians 9:25, 1 Peter 5:4).

iv. We are promised the *crown of life* if we will endure temptation (James 1:12).

v. Some people wonder if we will walk around heaven with crowns on, and everyone will notice who has the bigger and better crowns. But in Revelation 4:10, the elders surrounding the throne of God take their crowns and cast them before Jesus – giving any trophy they have received right back to Jesus.

b. **Which the Lord, the righteous Judge, will give to me on that Day**: Paul envisioned an awards ceremony where he would receive the crown that waited for him. Paul was about to be condemned and executed by an earthly court, but he was also going to be rewarded by a heavenly Lord.

i. "This is most probably the last letter the apostle ever wrote and it is impossible to see him in a more advantageous point of view than he now appears, standing on the verge of eternity, full of God, and strongly anticipating an eternity of glory." (Clarke)

ii. Some feel that Paul was too focused on rewards and that it isn't proper for Christians to think much about the reward they will receive in heaven. Yet God has no problem motivating us with heavenly reward. It *will* be worth it. We *must* hang in there now. We *will* be rewarded.

iii. Some Christians worry unnecessarily about their crown:

- What if I don't get a crown?
- What if my crown is really small?
- What if the Lord is disappointed in me?

iv. We should ignore all these speculations and simply be busy serving and glorifying God and our crown will take care of itself.

c. **Also to all who have loved His appearing**: This promise is for us – *if* we will set our focus on heaven and on the Jesus who both walked the earth and now reigns in heaven, who is waiting to receive us.

C. Paul's last words from prison.

1. (9-13) The solitude of the great apostle.

Be diligent to come to me quickly; for Demas has forsaken me, having loved this present world, and has departed for Thessalonica—Crescens for Galatia, Titus for Dalmatia. Only Luke is with me. Get Mark and bring him with you, for he is useful to me for ministry. And Tychicus I have sent to Ephesus. Bring the cloak that I left with Carpus at Troas when you come—and the books, especially the parchments.

a. **Be diligent to come to me quickly**: Paul was a man of God but he was not superhuman. He needed and wanted companionship. Paul was lonely.

b. **For Demas has forsaken me**: Paul remembers those who have forsaken him. Some (like **Demas**) left him because they had **loved this present world** (literally, "the now age"). Others left him out of necessity (like **Crescens** and **Titus**). Some other left because Paul sent them (like **Tychicus**).

i. Demas was mentioned in Paul's earlier letters as a fellow worker but later he went astray (Colossians 4:14 and Philemon 24). His previous faithfulness made it all more painful for Paul.

c. **Only Luke is with me**: Luke, who had traveled with Paul on many of his missionary journeys, remained with Paul. Everyone else was gone. This was a significant contrast to Paul's first Roman imprisonment ten years before, where he received many visitors (Acts 28:30-31).

d. **Get Mark and bring him with you**: This is evidence of a restoration of trust in Mark from Paul. Paul had wanted nothing to do with him in Acts 15:36-40.

e. **Bring the cloak that I left with Carpus at Troas**: This tells us that it is likely that Paul was arrested at Troas, resulting in this second imprisonment at Rome. In those days the arresting soldiers had claim to any extra garments in the possession of the one arrested. It may be that Paul was forewarned of the arrest and therefore committed his few books and this **cloak** – an outer garment – to the care of an honest man named **Carpus**.

i. The **cloak** was "A circular cape which fell down below the knees, with an opening for the head in the centre." (White)

ii. This cloak left in Troas shows us:

* Paul gave up everything to serve Jesus (all he had at the end of his life was a cloak and a few books).

* Paul was almost completely forsaken by his friends (he apparently had no friends to lend or obtain a cloak for him in Rome).

* Paul had a very independent mind (he would not beg for a cloak).

* Paul did not care much for how he was dressed (he could have asked for more or for different articles of clothing).

* Paul was an ordinary man with ordinary needs.

iii. "Oh, what a small deal of household stuff had this great apostle, saith Erasmus; a cloak to keep off the rain, and a few books and writings." (Trapp)

f. **And the books, especially the parchments**: Paul stayed a scholar to the end and wanted his books. He especially wanted the **parchments**, which were portions of the Old Testament.

i. "Still more does this passage refute the madness of the fanatics who despise books and condemn all reading and boast only of ... their private inspirations by God. But we should note that this passage commends continual reading to all godly men as a thing from which they can profit." (Calvin)

3. (14-15) A warning to beware of Alexander the coppersmith.

Alexander the coppersmith did me much harm. May the Lord repay him according to his works. You also must beware of him, for he has greatly resisted our words.

a. **Alexander the coppersmith did me much harm**: In 1 Timothy 1:20 Paul mentioned *Alexander* as someone who whose faith had suffered shipwreck. Now Paul warned Timothy about this same man. Paul simply wrote that Alexander **did me much harm** – but that he would also oppose Timothy (**You also must beware of him**).

   i. It would have been wrong of Timothy to respond to this by saying to Paul, "Paul, Alexander has always been nice to me. He has his faults, but don't we all?" Instead, we can be sure that Timothy respected Paul's judgment – and took his counsel to **beware of** Alexander.

   ii. **Coppersmith** "Does not mean that he worked only in copper. The term came to be used of workers in any kind of metal." (White)

b. **Did me much harm**: The implication of this phrase is that he "informed many things against me." Perhaps Alexander was a traitor, an informer who betrayed Paul to the Roman government and was responsible for his current imprisonment. Perhaps the thought of **he has greatly resisted our words** meant that Alexander was a witness against Paul at his first defense.

   i. "Informers were one of the great curses of Rome at this time. And it may well be that Alexander was a renegade Christian, who went to the magistrates with false information against Paul, seeking to ruin him in the most dishonourable way." (Barclay)

   ii. "They were accused to 'atheism,' (because they eschewed idolatry and emperor-worship), of cannibalism (because they spoke of eating Christ's body), and even of a general 'hatred of the human race' (because of their supposed disloyalty to Caesar and perhaps because they had renounced the popular pleasures of sin). It may be that some of these charges were being leveled against Paul." (Stott)

c. **May the Lord repay him according to his works**: Alexander's judgment would be simple. It is a terrible thing to be judged according to one's **works**.

i. "This is neither a curse nor a railing speech, saith an ancient, but a prediction well beseeming an apostle, that avenged not himself, but rather gave place to wrath, Romans 12:19." (Trapp)

4. (16-18) God's faithfulness to Paul at his first defense.

At my first defense no one stood with me, but all forsook me. May it not be charged against them. But the Lord stood with me and strengthened me, so that the message might be preached fully through me, and *that* all the Gentiles might hear. And I was delivered out of the mouth of the lion. And the Lord will deliver me from every evil work and preserve *me* for His heavenly kingdom. To Him *be* glory forever and ever. Amen!

a. **No one stood with me... But the Lord stood with me**: Paul was all alone, but Jesus stood by him and Paul served God faithfully during his first defense.

i. The words "**May it not be charged against them**" show that Paul was not bitter that **all forsook** him. This is powerful evidence of a great work of grace and spiritual maturity.

ii. Paul's **first defense** may have been his first imprisonment in Rome (spoken of at the end of Acts), or it could have been a first hearing under his current imprisonment.

b. **And I was delivered out of the mouth of the lion**: God had delivered Paul before so he had no doubt about God's power or goodness. Paul just didn't know if this time his fate would end with be **delivered out of the mouth of the lion** or being preserved **for His heavenly kingdom**.

c. **To Him be glory forever and ever**: This reflects an unreasonable optimism and joy. Paul faced his last moments of this life and he was, but many accounts, penniless, friendless, without valuable possessions, cold, without adequate clothing, and destined for a soon death. Yet, especially knowing the heavenly reward waiting for him, he would not trade his place with anyone.

5. (19-21) Paul's closing greetings to his friends in contact with Timothy, and from Roman Christians.

Greet Prisca and Aquila, and the household of Onesiphorus. Erastus stayed in Corinth, but Trophimus I have left in Miletus sick. Do your utmost to come before winter. Eubulus greets you, as well as Pudens, Linus, Claudia, and all the brethren.

a. **Greet Prisca and Aquila, and the household of Onesiphorus**: In his parting words, Paul's heart was for the people he knew. He thought about others and not himself. Paul knew the nature of Jesus and was an others-centered person just as Jesus was.

b. **Trophimus I have left in Miletus sick**: Paul was a man used by God to perform remarkable miracles of healing (such as in Acts 14:8-10 and 19:11-20), yet he left Trophimus **sick**. This shows that even the Apostle Paul did not have miraculous healing powers to use at his own will. He could only give a gift of healing if God it was God's will and timing.

i. Charles Spurgeon preached a whole sermon on the words **but Trophimus I have left in Miletus sick** (*The Sick Man Left Behind*). The points were:

- It is the will of God that some good men should be in ill health.

- Good men may be laid aside when they seem to be most needed.

- Good men would have the Lord's work go on whatever becomes of them.

ii. "It is possible that Erastus and Trophimus were with St. Paul when he was arrested the second time, and that they remained in his company as far as Miletus and Corinth respectively." (White)

c. **Do your utmost to come before winter**: This has much heart and emotion behind it. As an old man, Paul dearly wanted to see his young associate before he laid down his life for his Lord. We don't know if Paul ever saw Timothy again, but we can be sure Timothy did his **utmost to come before winter**.

i. Paul's imprisonment in the Mamertine prison (a bleak building still standing in Rome, built 100 years before Paul's imprisonment for political enemies of Rome) lasted until he was beheaded under Nero outside Rome's Ostian Gate at a place called "Three Fountains."

ii. An absurd legend was eventually spun that said that when Paul was beheaded, his severed head bounced three times and at each place it hit the ground a fountain sprung up – one hot, one warm, and the third cold – thus the place was called "Three Fountains."

iii. Paul was martyred in the aftermath of the great fires that swept Rome in A.D. 64 – which Nero, in some manner, tried to blame on Christians. According to some traditions, he was beheaded on the same day Peter was crucified upside-down. Paul was a Roman citizen and could not be legally crucified.

6. (22) The last words from the pen of Paul.

The Lord Jesus Christ be with your spirit. Grace be with you. Amen.

a. **The Lord Jesus Christ be with your spirit. Grace be with you**. The last words of Paul reflect a man who simply loved Jesus and had received His grace. This simplicity, and all the power that went with it, marked the entire ministry of Paul.

i. "Here a very close personal association between the Lord and Timothy is prayed for." (White)

b. **Amen**: Paul invited Timothy to affirm all this by an agreeing "**Amen**." Paul had fulfilled his ministry and was ready to receive his reward, and he wanted Timothy to do the same.

Titus 1 - A Mission for Titus

A. Introduction and greeting.

1. (1) The Apostle Paul, author of this letter to Titus.

Paul, a bondservant of God and an apostle of Jesus Christ, according to the faith of God's elect and the acknowledgment of the truth which accords with godliness,

a. **Paul**: In writing his own name first, Paul followed the letter-writing customs of his day. First the writer was mentioned, and then the reader, and then a greeting was given.

i. From Titus 1:5 we learn that Paul and Titus worked together in Crete, spreading the gospel and establishing churches – but Paul had to leave. Titus stayed and worked among the congregations there. Since Titus was left behind to do a difficult work, Paul wanted to instruct and encourage him – and he did so with this letter.

ii. "That St. Paul had been in Crete, though nowhere else intimated, is clear from this passage. That he could not have made such an important visit, and evangelized an island of the first consequence, without it being mentioned by his historian, Luke, had it happened during the period embraced in the Acts of the Apostles, must be evident. That the journey, therefore, must have been performed *after* the time in which St. Luke ends his history, that is, after St. Paul's first imprisonment at Rome, seems almost certain." (Clarke)

iii. Paul wrote this as two other Christian workers (*Zenas* and *Apollos*, mentioned in Titus 3:13) were about to go to Crete, so Paul sent this letter with them.

iv. This letter was written to Titus, but it was also written to the Christians on the island of Crete. Paul knew this letter would be publicly read among the churches on the island. So, in the structure of opening the letter, Paul took great care to tell the Christians of Crete *what* his credentials were, and *where* he stood on important issues. Paul didn't think like a politician who often responds to what the crowd wants and to what pleases the crowd.

b. **Paul, a bondservant of God**: Of all the titles Paul could use, he first chose "**bondservant of God**." If Paul had a modern-day business card, that would be his title on the card.

  i. Significantly, when Paul used the term **bondservant**, he chose the ancient Greek word *doulos*. This word not only designated a *low* slave (one Greek scholar called it "the most abject, servile term in use among the Greeks for a slave"), it was also the word for a slave by *choice*.

  ii. Paul was only a **bondservant** - yet he had a high place, because He was **a bondservant of God**. It is never a low thing to be a servant of a great God.

c. **And an apostle of Jesus Christ**: God gave Paul a special role to play among His servants. Paul's particular call and function was as a special messenger of God - **an apostle**. Paul knew his call and purpose among the body of Christ, and so should each Christian today also know for themselves.

d. **According to the faith**: Paul wasn't an apostle *because* of the faith of God's elect, but in harmony with **the faith** (in the sense of a specific, common body of doctrine) shared among **God's elect**.

  i. **God's elect** are those whom He chose from before the foundation of the world to receive His salvation. We can identify **God's elect** because they respond to the gospel of Jesus Christ and live their lives after that gospel.

e. **The acknowledgement of the truth**: For Paul it wasn't enough to just *know* the faith, he also had to *acknowledge* it for what it really was.

f. **Which accords with godliness**: Paul stood in accord with godly living. All truth is God's truth; but not all truth is really relevant to **godliness**, which promotes "God-likeness". Much of science or psychology may be true and admirable - but it won't save a soul from Hell. It is not **the truth which accords with godliness**.

2. (2) Paul was an apostle in the **hope of eternal life**.

In hope of eternal life which God, who cannot lie, promised before time began,

  a. **Eternal life**: This is the life of the Eternal God living within us. It is present now, but will be completed later.

i. "The Christian gospel does not in the first place offer men an intellectual creed or a moral code; it offers them life, the very life of God." (Barclay)

b. **Which God, who cannot lie, promised**: This eternal life is not a *wish*, but a **hope**. In this sense, **hope** is an anticipation founded not on wishful thinking, but on a promise from the **God who cannot lie**.

3. (3) Paul was an apostle who believed in preaching the word.

But has in due time manifested His word through preaching, which was committed to me according to the commandment of God our Savior;

a. **But in due time manifested His word through preaching**: Paul knew that **preaching** is the way that God's eternal work meets people today. **Preaching** is the way God's word is made evident (**manifested**).

i. **But has in due time manifested His word**: Christianity came into the world at a time when it was uniquely possible for its message to spread rapidly.

- There was a common language (Greek), which was the language of trade, business, and literature.

- There were virtually no frontiers because of the vast nature of the Roman Empire.

- Travel was comparatively easy. It was slow, but relatively safe because of the security that the Roman Empire brought to roads and sea routes.

- The world was largely at peace under the *pax Romana*.

- The world was uniquely conscious of its need for a messiah and savior. "There was never a time when the hearts of men were more open to receive the message of salvation which the Christian missionaries brought." (Barclay)

b. **Which was committed to me**: Paul knew the work of preaching was entrusted to him, but not to him only. Preaching is a work committed to all believers.

4. (4) The reader: Titus, Paul's convert and his **true** (faithful) **son**.

To Titus, a true son in *our* common faith: Grace, mercy, *and* peace from God the Father and the Lord Jesus Christ our Savior.

a. **To Titus**: Significantly, we don't know anything about Titus from Acts. He is strangely absent from that record, though he must have been an associate of Paul during the time covered by Acts. Yet we do read about him in 2 Corinthians 2:13, 8:23, and 12:18.

i. "2 Corinthians 8:18 and 2 Corinthians 12:18 both say that when Titus was sent to Corinth another brother was sent with him, described in the former passage as 'the brother who is famous among all the churches,' and commonly identified with Luke. It has been suggested that Titus was Luke's brother." (Barclay)

ii. Though we read nothing about Titus in Acts, we still know something of his character and personality.

- Titus was a **true son in our common faith** (Titus 1:4).

- Titus was a genuine *brother* to the Apostle Paul (2 Corinthians 2:13).

- Titus was a *partner and a fellow worker* with Paul (2 Corinthians 8:23).

- Titus walked *in the same spirit* as Paul (2 Corinthians 12:18).

- Titus walked *in the same steps* as Paul, in the same manner of life (2 Corinthians 12:18).

- Therefore, Titus could be a *pattern* to other believers (Titus 2:7).

iii. "He seems to have been a man of great common sense; so that, when Paul had anything difficult to be done, he sent Titus. When the collection was to be made at Corinth on behalf of the poor saints at Jerusalem, Paul sent Titus to stir the members up, and with him another brother to take charge of the contributions." (Spurgeon)

b. **A true son in our common faith**: Paul stood in support of a **common faith**. It is a **common** faith, not an isolated one. Paul was for the church and the community of all believers.

i. "It must not be restricted to a faith shared only by St. Paul and Titus; but, like [Jude 3], it is common to all Christians." (White)

c. **Grace, mercy, and peace**: In his greeting Paul used words typical for a greeting in the ancient world. But when Paul used these words, they were not used just as a formality because Paul knew the *source* of all **grace, mercy, and peace**. They come **from God the Father and the Lord Jesus Christ our Savior**.

i. God the Father and God the Son share in the gift of salvation. "The Son has brought to us salvation from the Father, and the Father has bestowed it through the Son." (Calvin)

B. Paul's mission for Titus.

1. (5) The challenge given to Titus.

For this reason I left you in Crete, that you should set in order the things that are lacking, and appoint elders in every city as I commanded you—

a. **For this reason I left you in Crete**: After a successful evangelistic campaign on the island of Crete, there were a lot of young Christians to take care of. Paul left Titus behind to build stable churches with mature, qualified pastors for the people. This was especially needed in Crete, because the people of Crete were a wild bunch, well known as liars and lazy people. Titus had to find and train capable leaders for the Christians of the island of Crete.

i. When a job is hard, there are basically two kinds of people. With one you say, "The job is really hard, so we can't send him." With the other you say, "The job is really hard, so we must send him." Titus seemed to be of the second kind.

ii. **I left you in Crete** uses the same wording as Paul used in 2 Timothy 4:13 and 4:20 where he spoke of a cloak and an associate temporarily left behind. The idea is that he left Titus in Crete on a limited basis to solve these problems, establish godly leadership, and then move on (probably to catch up again with Paul).

b. **Set in order the things that are lacking**: This was the job Titus was given. The church needed order and leadership. Titus was commanded to **set in order** the churches, and to do it by appointing godly leaders.

i. "That phrase is a medical term; it was applied to the setting of a crooked limb." (Wiersbe) There were crooked things that had to be set straight among the congregations of Crete.

ii. If we compare the work of Titus in Crete to the work of Timothy in Ephesus (as shown by 1 and 2 Timothy), it shows there was much more **lacking** among the congregations of Crete. Paul specifically told Titus to **set in order the things that are lacking** and gave no such command to Timothy.

iii. Apparently the Ephesian congregations were ready for both elders and deacons, but only elders are mentioned in Titus.

c. **And appoint elders in every city**: Paul told Titus to **appoint elders**, who are also called bishops in Titus 1:7. The word *elder* is used broadly in the New Testament, mainly describing the maturity necessary in leaders. **Elders** and *bishops* describe pastors over congregations in different cities on Crete.

i. "The number of presbyters is not specified; the meaning is that the order of presbyters should be established all over the island." (White)

ii. **As I commanded you**: "In the phrase *as I had appointed thee* (RSV better 'as I directed you') the *I* is emphatic, bringing out not Paul's egotism, but his authoritative endorsement of the elder-system." (Guthrie)

d. **In every city**: This was a big job, because Crete was famous for having many cities.

i. "It should be carefully noted that churches cannot safely remain without the ministry of pastors, so that, wherever there is a considerable body of people, a pastor should be appointed over them. In saying that each town should have a pastor he does not mean that none should have more than one, but only that no town should be without pastors." (Calvin)

e. **Appoint elders**: This means Paul delegated a lot of authority to Titus. These elders were not chosen by popular vote, and they were not chosen through their own self-promotion. It was Titus' job to look for men of the kind of character Paul would describe in the following passage and to **appoint** them as **elders** in congregations.

i. Calvin notes that this means Paul gave Titus a tremendous amount of authority, and that under Paul's direction (and the direction of the Holy Spirit), this authority was in Titus and not in a group or a committee. "But he may seem to give Titus too much authority when he tells him to appoint ministers for all the churches. This would be almost royal power and would deprive individual churches of their right to elect and the college of pastors of their right to judge, and that would be to profane the whole administration of the Church." (Calvin)

ii. Calvin goes on to suggest that the answer is easy – that Titus actually just approved or ratified the leaders that the congregations themselves selected. *There is not a hint of this in the text of Titus or anywhere else.* Plainly, God intended Titus as one man to have this authority and for him to use it in a godly manner.

iii. The list in the following passage means that God has specific *qualifications* for leaders in the church. Leaders should not to be chosen at random, or just because they volunteer, or because they aspire to the position, or even because they are "natural leaders." Leaders should be chosen because they match the qualifications listed here. It is fine if a man thinks he is "called." Yet he must also be *qualified*.

iv. The qualifications for leadership in the following passage have nothing to do with *giftedness*. Paul didn't say to Titus "Find the most gifted guys." We might say that it is easy for the Lord to grant gifts by the Holy Spirit as He wills (1 Corinthians 12:11), but developing character takes time and a real relationship with Jesus Christ.

- Going to seminary doesn't make one qualified for spiritual leadership.

- Being a good talker doesn't make one qualified for spiritual leadership.

- Natural or spiritual gifts in themselves do not qualify one for spiritual leadership.

- What one gives in money or volunteer time does not qualify them for spiritual leadership.

- What qualifies a man for spiritual leadership is *godly character* - and godly character established according to the clear criteria Paul will list.

v. However, this is not a rigid list which demands *perfection* in all areas. It provides both goals to reach for and general criteria for selection. We should take this list and ask "Does the man in question desire all these things with his whole heart? Does that desire show itself in his life?" Titus was to take the following list, find the men who *best* fit the description, and then use the list as a training guide to disciple these men.

vi. As well, these qualifications are valuable for every person - not only those who aspire to leadership. They are clear indicators of godly character and spiritual maturity; they can give a true measure of a man.

3. (6-8) What Titus must look for in the appointment of leaders.

If a man is blameless, the husband of one wife, having faithful children not accused of dissipation or insubordination. For a bishop must be blameless, as a steward of God, not self-willed, not quick-tempered, not given to wine, not violent, not greedy for money, but hospitable, a lover of what is good, sober-minded, just, holy, self-controlled,

a. **If a man is blameless**: This word literally means "nothing to take hold upon." There must be nothing in the life of the leader that others can take hold of and attack his life or the church.

i. This is a broad term for a man who lives a righteous life that can be *seen* as righteous. No one could stand up and rightfully accuse the man of grievous sin.

ii. This is important, because he was **a steward of** God's house. The greater the master is, the greater the servants are expected to be.

b. **Husband of one wife**: The idea is of "a one-woman man." It does not mean that a leader *must* be married. If that were the case, then both Jesus and Paul would be disqualified from leadership. Nor is it the idea that a leader could never remarry if his wife had passed away or if he were Biblically divorced. The idea is that the leader has his focus upon one woman – that being his wife.

c. **Having faithful children**: The leader must have raised his children well. His ability to lead the family of God must be first demonstrated by his ability to lead his own children. Here the emphasis is on the idea that his children are believers also.

> i. "If they remained pagans, it would throw into question the father's ability to lead others to the faith." (Hiebert) "A wise father first wins his own family to Christ and then gives them a chance to grow before he pulls up stakes and moves to bible school. We would have fewer casualties in the ministry if this policy were followed more often." (Wiersbe)

> ii. "It is significant that the moral requirements of the pastor's children are more mildly expressed in 1 Timothy 3:4,5,12. There it is the father's power to keep order in his own house that is emphasised; here the submission of the children to discipline and restraint." (White)

> iii. "The family of the elder must be such that they cannot be accused of [**dissipation**]. The Greek word is *asotia*. It is the word used in Luke 15:13 for the *riotous* living of the prodigal son. The man who is *asotos* is incapable of saving; he is wasteful and extravagant and pours out his substance on personal pleasure; he destroys his substance and in the end ruins himself." (Barclay)

d. **Not self-willed**: Basically, selfish people are disqualified from leadership. They show their **self-willed** nature in arrogance, stubbornness, and a proud self-focus.

> i. "Not one who is determined to have his own way in every thing; setting up his own judgment to that of all others; expecting all to pay homage to his understanding." (Clarke)

e. **Not quick-tempered**: The **quick-tempered** are also disqualified from leadership, as are those who drink more than is proper (**not given to wine**), the **violent**, and those **greedy for money**.

> i. **Not quick-tempered**: The ancient Greek word used here (*orgilos*) actually refers more to *a settled state of anger* than the flash of an occasional bad temper. It speaks of a man who has a constant simmering

anger and who nourishes his anger against others – close to the idea of a *bitter* man.

ii. **Violent**: "The Greeks themselves widened the meaning of this word to include, not only violence in action, but also violence in speech. The word came to mean one who *browbeats* his fellow-men, and it may well be that it should be so translated here." (Barclay)

iii. **Not greedy for money**: "There are no regulations here laid down for deacons; so we are entitled to conclude that in Crete, at this time, presbyters performed the duties of every church office. Hence they should have the appropriate deaconal virtue [as in 1 Timothy 3:8]." (White)

f. **But hospitable**: A leader among God's people must be a **hospitable** man, and one who loves **what is good**. Men who love the base and the sordid things of this world are not yet qualified to be leaders among God's people.

g. **Sober-minded**: This describes the person who is *able to think clearly and with clarity*. They are not constant joke-makers but know how to deal with serious subjects in a serious way.

i. Wiersbe on **soberminded**: "This does not man he has no sense of humor, or that he is always solemn and somber. Rather it suggests that he knows the value of things and does not cheapen the ministry or the Gospel message by foolish behavior." (From Wiersbe's commentary on 1 Timothy)

ii. In the mind of the Apostle Paul, this was an *important* quality in a leader. He used this word ten times in his short letters to Timothy and Titus.

h. **Just, holy, self-controlled**: A pastor or leader in the church must be **just** (right toward men), **holy** (right towards God), **self-controlled** (right towards himself).

i. "How unfit are those to govern a church who cannot govern themselves!" (Matthew Henry)

C. What leaders in the church are supposed to do.

1. (9a) Titus must appoint elders who will hold fast to the word of God.

Holding fast the faithful word as he has been taught,

a. **Holding fast the faithful word**: This means first that the leader must be sure of the **faithful word** for himself. When he brings the word of God to people he must bring it with confidence and authority, not mixed with theological speculation and academic doubts.

i. "There is not need of fancy words, but of strong minds, of skill in the scriptures, and of powerful thoughts." (Chrysostom)

b. **Holding fast the faithful word**: This means also that the leader will *stick* to God's word, instead of a focus on fads and programs for the church. If a man will not first stick *to* the word and will not then stick *with* the word of God, he is not qualified for leadership in God's church.

c. **As he has been taught**: This means that the leader has *been under* the teaching of someone else. A qualified leader doesn't necessarily need to go to Bible College or Seminary, but they do need to be **taught** and discipled by *someone*, not just themselves.

2. (9b) Titus must appoint leaders who will also *use* the word properly.

That he may be able, by sound doctrine, both to exhort and convict those who contradict.

a. **That he may be able... both to exhort and convict those who contradict**: A godly leader will use his solid foundation in God's word to **exhort** (encourage) those who are on the right track. He will also use it to **convict** (discourage) those who are on the wrong track, **those who contradict**.

i. "A preacher must be both soldier and shepherd. He must nourish, defend, and teach; he must have teeth in his mouth and be able to bite and fight." (Luther)

b. **By sound doctrine**: A godly leader deals with **those who contradict**, and he does it with **sound doctrine**. He doesn't do it with pompous authority and political backstabbing. He brings correction with **sound doctrine**.

i. If a leader does not have a basis in **sound doctrine** to either **exhort** or **convict** an individual, he probably shouldn't do it. Leaders need to stand on the foundation of the word.

D. Why it was important for Titus to appoint these qualified leaders.

1. (10-11) Those who must be confronted and how to stop them.

For there are many insubordinate, both idle talkers and deceivers, especially those of the circumcision, whose mouths must be stopped, who subvert whole households, teaching things which they ought not, for the sake of dishonest gain.

a. **For there are many insubordinate**: The word **insubordinate** indicates someone who will not submit to God's order of authority. The ancient Greek word translated **insubordinate** is the negative form of the word *submit* - an **insubordinate** man will not submit.

i. God has established an order of authority in several different areas of life. There is an order of authority in the home, in the church, in the workplace, and in the community. God wants us to recognize the places where He has place an order of authority in our lives, and He wants us to submit to that authority.

ii. If there were many contentious and "problem people" among God's people in Paul's day, so soon after the apostle himself had been among them, then we should also expect that there would be such people today. There are still **many insubordinate**.

b. **Idle talkers and deceivers**: These problem people will make themselves known by their unwise speech and by their deception.

i. **Idle talkers**: "The main idea was of a worship which produced no goodness of life. These people in Crete could talk glibly but all their talk was ineffective in bringing anyone one step nearer goodness." (Barclay)

c. **Especially those of the circumcision**: Paul was particularly concerned with the effect of some Christians from a Jewish background, who thought the key to acceptance before God was keeping the Law of Moses.

i. The words **insubordinate** and **of the circumcision** taken together show that these were Christians from a Jewish background, or at least they were Christians in name. "We cannot call those persons *unruly* on whose obedience we have no claim." (White)

ii. "They tried to persuade them that the simple story of Jesus and the Cross was not sufficient, but that, to be really wise, they needed all the subtle stories and the long genealogies and the elaborate allegories of the Rabbis. Further, they tried to teach them that grace was not enough, but that, to be really good, they needed to take upon themselves all the rules and regulations about foods and washings which were so characteristic of Judaism." (Barclay)

iii. We can understand why it might be more difficult for Christians who came from Judaism and why they might tend to be more of a source of trouble in the early churches. Christians from pagan backgrounds immediately knew that they had to reject everything about their prior understanding about the gods. Yet Christians from Judaism had to take some things and leave others, and this is often more difficult.

d. **Whose mouths must be stopped**: Titus had to train the elders he chose to simply "shut up" these problem people. They should not to be allowed to gain a hearing, because if allowed, they would **subvert whole households**.

i. **Whose mouths must be stopped**: "That does not imply that they are to be silence by violence or persecution… it became the normal word for *to silence a person by reason*." (Barclay)

e. **Teaching things which they ought not**: There are at least three things which should not be taught among Christians. First, *false doctrine* **ought not** to be taught. Second, **insubordinate** things **ought not** to be taught. Third, *unprofitable* things **ought not** to be taught.

i. In 1 Timothy 1:4, Paul warned Timothy to not *give heed to fables and endless genealogies, which cause disputes rather than godly edification which is in faith*. There are certain spiritual subjects that are not edifying, and are not profitable. All they do is cause speculations and arguments. When Titus found men **teaching things which they ought not**, he was supposed to stop it.

f. **For the sake of dishonest gain**: These problem people were motivated by **gain**. Paul's main idea was of dishonest financial gain, and there are many who fit that description today. However, the **dishonest gain** some seek from the gospel is emotional instead of financial. They serve for the sake of the **gain** that comes when others recognize or admire them as a spiritual leader.

2. (12-14) Why the problem is difficult, and what to do about it.

One of them, a prophet of their own, said, "Cretans *are* always liars, evil beasts, lazy gluttons." This testimony is true. Therefore rebuke them sharply, that they may be sound in the faith, not giving heed to Jewish fables and commandments of men who turn from the truth.

a. **Cretans are always liars, evil beasts, lazy gluttons**: The problem was difficult because of the general character of the **Cretans**. Even prophets among the Cretans described the island people as **liars, evil beasts,** and **lazy gluttons**, it indicates that there is a character problem.

i. If the Cretans had this basic character, it shows *why* it was so important for Titus to appoint elders to lead the church. If these congregations were left to themselves, chaos and error would dominate the churches.

ii. **A prophet of their own**: Paul did not mean that the Cretan writer he quotes here was an inspired prophet of God. But that writer did have it correct when he described the character of the people of Crete. As Paul wrote, *this* **testimony** - not the *entire* testimony of this writer - **is true**.

iii. "There was a Cretan prophet once who told plain truths to his countrymen. The whole line occurs, according to Jerome, in the [works] of Epimenides, a native of Cnossus in Crete." (White)

iv. "So notorious were the Cretans that the Greeks actually formed a verb *kretizein, to cretize,* which means *to lie and to cheat;* and they had a proverbial phrase, *kreitzein pros Kreta,* to cretize against a Cretan, which meant to *match lies with lies,* as diamond cuts diamond." (Barclay)

v. Paul didn't say to Titus, "Cretans are liars and cheats and gluttons, with one of the worst reputations of any group in the Roman Empire. You should look for an easier group to work with." Instead he said, "I know how bad they are. Go out and change them with the power of Jesus and for His glory."

b. **Therefore rebuke them sharply**: Because of the generally hardened character of the people of the island of Crete, they must be dealt with directly. Titus himself must **rebuke them sharply, that they may be sound in the faith,** and he must also appoint leaders who will do the same.

c. **Not giving heed to Jewish fables and commandments of men who turn from the truth**: As mentioned before (*especially those of the circumcision,* Titus 1:10) the particular point of contention in the churches of Crete had to do with a Jewish legalism. It was not centered not on God's word, but on **Jewish fables and the commandments of men who turn from the truth**.

3. (15-16) The character of these difficult people.

To the pure all things are pure, but to those who are defiled and unbelieving nothing is pure; but even their mind and conscience are defiled. They profess to know God, but in works they deny Him, being abominable, disobedient, and disqualified for every good work.

a. **To the pure, all things are pure**: With their attraction to Jewish legalism, the difficult people Titus had to confront seemed to believe that **nothing is pure**. They denied Christians basic and godly pleasures that were not sin.

i. Timothy had to deal with the same kind of people. Paul warned Timothy about those *forbidding to marry, and commanding to abstain from foods which God created to be received with thanksgiving by those who believe and know the truth* (1 Timothy 4:3). Paul knew that if a Christian walked in the purity of the Lord, these things were **pure** to him. But to those of a legalistic mind (**those who are defiled and unbelieving**), they seemed to believe **nothing is pure**. The problem was with their **defiled and unbelieving** minds and consciences, not with the things themselves.

ii. **All things are pure**: Of course, Paul does not mean that obviously sinful things (pornography, illicit drugs, and the like) **are pure**. Paul has in mind those things which are permitted by Scripture, but forbidden by legalists in a mistaken attempt to earn favor with God.

iii. "Paul was refuting the false teaching of these legalists with reference to *foods*. They were teaching that Jewish dietary laws still applied to Christian believers." (Wiersbe)

iv. "The 'all things' refers to everything which is non-moral; such as appetite and food, desire and marriage, exchange and commerce, weariness and recreation, and so on through all the varied realm of life. To the pure all these things are pure, and they will be maintained in purity. To the impure, every one of them may be made the vehicle and occasion of impurity." (Morgan)

b. **They profess to know God, but in works they deny Him**: These difficult people Titus had to deal with were all the more difficult because they *talked* like Christians. Their *profession* was all in order, but **in works they deny Him**. We can't just go by what a person *says*. We have to also look at how they *live*.

i. "They acted as if this Supreme Being was a mere metaphysical abstraction, out of all moral relation to human life, as if He were neither Saviour nor Judge." (J.H. Bernard, cited in White)

c. **Being abominable, disobedient, and disqualified for every good work**: These are strong words, but Paul means it. These difficult people probably pretended to have a higher spirituality than Titus or other godly leaders. But Paul saw right through their spiritual façade and wanted Titus - and all the Christians on Crete - to see through it also.

i. The word **abominable** has the idea of *polluted by idolatry*.

ii. **Disqualified**: The ancient Greek word is *adokimos*, and was used in many different ways:

- It was used to describe a counterfeit coin.
- It was used to describe a cowardly soldier who failed in battle.
- It was used of a candidate rejected for elected office.
- It was used of stone rejected by builders. If a stone had a bad enough flaw, it was marked with a capital A (for *adokimos*) and set aside as unfit.

Titus 2 - Teach Them How to Live

"FEW portions of the New Testament excel this chapter. It may well form the creed, system of ethics, and text book of every Christian preacher. Does any man inquire what is the duty of a Gospel minister? Send him to the second chapter of the Epistle to Titus for a complete answer." (Adam Clarke)

A. How Titus must teach different groups of people in the church.

1. (1) The command to teach.

But as for you, speak the things which are proper for sound doctrine:

a. **But as for you**: This sets Titus apart from the people described at the end of Titus 1. They may teach legalism and fables, but Titus was to teach **the things which are proper for sound doctrine**.

b. **Things which are proper for sound doctrine**: The idea behind this phrase has to do with *right living*, not just *right thinking*. The Living Bible translates this "Speak up for the right living that goes along with true Christianity." The New Living Translation has "Promote the kind of living that reflects right teaching."

i. We can't escape it. The Bible is a book that tells us how to *live*. It is the height of hypocrisy to say that we believe its truth if we ignore how it tells us to live our lives. We don't always like it, but we always need to hear how God expects us to *live*.

ii. Paul simply wants Titus to fulfill the command of Jesus in Matthew 28:19-20: *Teaching them to observe all things that I have commanded you.*

2. (2) What to teach the older men.

That the older men be sober, reverent, temperate, sound in faith, in love, in patience;

a. **The older men**: Titus had some **older men** among the Christians in Crete. They had to be approached with love and wisdom, or they might easily be offended when taught by a younger man like Titus.

b. **Older men**: Paul wanted Titus to know that they must live with the maturity and wisdom that their years should give them. This means **sober, reverent,** and **temperate** lives. The command to teach these things means that they do not come *automatically* with age.

c. **Older men**: They must also have stability, being stable in the right things: **sound in faith, in love, in patience**. As we get older, we tend to "harden" in our ways. This is a good thing if we "harden" in the ways of **faith, love,** and **patience**.

i. **Patience** is the great ancient Greek word *hupomone*. It means a steadfast and active endurance, not a passive waiting. **Older men** are not to just patiently wait around until they pass on to the next world. They are to actively endure the challenges of life; even the challenges of old age.

4. (3-4a) How to teach the older women.

The older women likewise, that they be reverent in behavior, not slanderers, not given to much wine, teachers of good things—that they admonish the young women

a. **The older women likewise**: Just as Titus had to give special consideration to the *older men*, also must he keep in mind how to approach the **older women**. They have their own set of temptations and opportunities.

b. **Reverent in behavior, not slanderers**: The idea behind **behavior** includes a suggestion of dress and how a woman carries herself. The word for **slanderers** is the same word used for "devils." When **the older women** - or anyone else, for that matter - slander and gossip, then they do the devils' work

i. "The adjective 'reverent' basically means 'suitable to a sacred office' and conveys the image of a good priestess carrying out the duties of her office. The conduct of the older women must reveal that they regard life as sacred in all of its aspects." (Hiebert)

c. **Not given to much wine**: This was a common failing of **older women** in Roman and Greek culture. Paul recognizes that this special challenge needs special instruction.

i. "The two prohibitions which follow, *not false accusers* and *not given to much wine*, again vividly portray the contemporary Cretan environment. The first has already been met in 1 Timothy 3:11

and the second in 1 Timothy 3:8. Evidently in Crete the liability to these excesses was more severe than in Ephesus, especially among the women, for the verb (*doulo*) used here signifies 'bondage' (RSV 'slaves to drink'), a much stronger expression than the corresponding phrase in 1 Timothy." (Guthrie)

d. **Teachers of good things**: If the **older women** have special challenges, they also have special opportunities. God can use their wisdom and experience as they **admonish the young women**. This gives the **older women** something *positive* to live towards, instead of the *negative* things of slander and alcohol abuse.

i. "To bring out the required Christian characteristics the apostle uses a unique compound expression, *kalodidaskaloi, teachers of good things*." (Guthrie)

4. (4b-5) How to teach the younger women.

The young women to love their husbands, to love their children, to be discreet, chaste, homemakers, good, obedient to their own husbands, that the word of God may not be blasphemed.

a. **The young women**: According to Paul's instruction, Titus was not to make it his ministry to teach the **young women** directly. Instead, he was to equip and encourage the *older women* to teach **the young women**.

i. Of course, this doesn't mean that **the young women** were barred from listening to Titus teach. It simply means that it was wrong - and dangerous - for Titus to make **the young women** a focus of his ministry. If there was a **young women** Bible Study group, Titus shouldn't teach it. The *older women* should.

b. **To love their husbands, to love their children**: Instruction for **the young women** begins with home matters. God has given them a strategic position of influence and assistance to **their husbands** and **their children**, and they must let **love** dominate their influence and assistance.

i. Paul says that **love** for husbands and children must be *taught*. Certainly, aspects of this love are inborn. But other aspects - especially aspects that reflect the self-giving sacrifice of Jesus - must be *taught*.

c. **To be discreet, chaste, homemakers**: The **young women** must be taught these *attitudes* (**discreet, chaste**) and *skills* (**homemakers**).

d. **Good, obedient to their own husbands**: *Goodness* isn't always easy in a world that blurs the line between good and evil, so the older women need to teach the younger to be **good. Obedient to their own husbands** is another way of expressing the wife's duty of submission in the marriage relationship (Ephesians 5:22, Colossians 3:18).

e. **That the word of God may not be blasphemed**: This shows *how important* it is for the older women to teach these things, and for the **younger women** to learn them. When Christians don't live in a Biblical, godly manner it means that the **word of God may** be **blasphemed** among the ungodly.

> i. "The practical worth of a religion is not unfairly estimated by its effects on the lives of those who profess it. If the observed effect of the Gospel were to make women worse wives, it would not commend it to the heathen." (White)

5. (6) How to teach the younger men.

Likewise exhort the young men to be sober-minded,

a. **Likewise**: This is a *linking* word. It shows that what the **young men** need to learn isn't all that different from what the younger women, the older women, and the older men need to learn. We may need a slightly different *emphasis* depending on our station in life, but the essential message of godly living is the same.

b. **To be sober-minded**: The Living Bible translates the thought well: *Urge the young men to behave carefully, taking life seriously.* This is the only command Titus is told to emphasize to **young men**, but sometimes a difficult one for younger men.

> i. **Sober-minded**: "The word is *sophron*, and it describes the man with the mind which has everything under control... strength of mind which has learned to govern every instinct and passion until each has its proper place and no more." (Barclay)

6. (7-8) Titus and his practical example to the young men.

In all things showing yourself *to be* a pattern of good works; in doctrine *showing* integrity, reverence, incorruptibility, sound speech that cannot be condemned, that one who is an opponent may be ashamed, having nothing evil to say of you.

a. **In all things showing yourself to be a pattern of good works**: Titus had to be more than a teacher, he also had to be an example. His guidance to others could not be taken seriously if he himself was not walking after the Lord.

b. **In doctrine showing integrity**: Titus had to be an example in doctrinal stability and integrity. If he wasn't comfortably settled in his understanding of the Scriptures, he wasn't ready to lead.

c. **That one who is an opponent may be ashamed**: So that your accusers will be embarrassed, having nothing to hold against you. Jesus could say to an angry mob, "Which of you convicts Me of sin?" (John 8:46)

i. White on **having nothing evil to say**: "The clause means *having nothing evil to report concerning us*: not, as the English versions, *having no evil thing to say*."

7. (9-10) How to teach servants.

Exhort bondservants to be obedient to their own masters, to be well pleasing in all *things*, not answering back, not pilfering, but showing all good fidelity, that they may adorn the doctrine of God our Savior in all things.

a. **Exhort bondservants**: Titus was to teach **bondservants** about their specific duties as Christians. In the ancient world, Christians shocked the larger culture by mixing slaves and masters in the social setting of the church service. This meant that a slave might go to church and be an elder over his own master.

i. "I do not think for a moment Paul believed that the practice of slavery ought to exist. He believed to the fullest extent that the great principles of Christianity would overthrow slavery anywhere, and the sooner they did so the better pleased would he be; but, for the time being, as it was the custom to have slaves, they must adorn the doctrine of God their Savior in the position in which they were." (Spurgeon)

b. **Obedient to their own masters**: Paul doesn't say that **bondservants** should **be obedient** to every free man, only to **their own masters**. This means that Paul recognized that **bondservants** had obligations, but only to **their own masters**.

i. **Obedient**: "The word 'obedient' was used to describe a company of soldiers as they stand at attention and salute their commander. They are declaring as they stand at attention in front of him that they are ready to take his orders." (Draper)

ii. At the same time, as in every arena of human submission, our obedience and submission is limited by our higher responsibility to obey God. As Peter said in Acts 5:29, *We ought to obey God rather than men* when there is a conflict between the two.

c. **Not pilfering**: This type of offence was so common in the ancient world that sometimes the words *servant* and *thief* were used interchangeably. It was assumed that servants would steal from their masters in these small ways.

i. **Pilfering**: "The word signifies, not only *stealing* but *embezzling* another's property; *keeping back a part of the price* of any commodity sold on the master's account. In Acts 5:2, we translate it, *to keep back part of the price*; the crime of which Ananias and Saphira were guilty." (Clarke)

d. **Well pleasing in all things**: Simply, Titus must direct servants to be good workers in all ways. By their hard work and humble submission, they will **adorn the doctrine of God our Savior**.

i. **Adorn**: "It literally means to take precious jewels and arrange them so as to show their true beauty." (Draper)

ii. In one sense the gospel doesn't need adornment. At the same time, we can *show* the beauty of the gospel by the way we live. We often think we need better *words* to adorn the gospel. Better words are fine, but what we really need are better *lives*.

iii. Wonderfully, those who (in this context) have the ability to **adorn the doctrine of God our Savior** are **bondservants** – slaves under a master. Even one in a low or disadvantaged station in life has the potential to beautify God's truth by the way they live.

iv. "Thus we see how 'the doctrine of God our Savior' may 'be adorned.' It is adorned when its effects on life and character are expressed in conduct.... While it is still only a theory doctrine lacks the manifestation of beauty. When, however, it is realized and manifested in human life its beauty at once appears. The value of a theory is always supremely apparent in the results it produces." (Morgan)

B. The place of grace in the Christian life.

1. (11) Saving grace.

For the grace of God that brings salvation has appeared to all men,

a. **The grace of God that brings salvation**: Grace *brings salvation*. You don't go out and "get" salvation; it comes to you and you have the opportunity to receive it.

b. **Has appeared to all men**: There is one gospel of grace for **all men**. God doesn't have a gospel of grace for some and a gospel of law or self-justification for others. **All men** find **salvation** by the **grace of God**.

i. "No rank or class or type of mankind is outside the saving influence of God's grace." (White)

ii. "There is a beauty and energy in the word *epiphaino, hath shined out*, that is rarely noted; it seems to be a metaphor taken from the *sun*. As by his rising in the east and *shining out*, he enlightens, *successively*, the whole world; so the Lord Jesus, who is called the *Sun of righteousness*, Malachi 4:2, arises on the whole human race with healing in his wings." (Clarke)

iii. The light and warmth of the sun is for the whole earth; but it does not shine upon the earth all at the same time, nor in the same intensity from place to place.

2. (12-13) What grace teaches us.

Teaching us that, denying ungodliness and worldly lusts, we should live soberly, righteously, and godly in the present age, looking for the blessed hope and glorious appearing of our great God and Savior Jesus Christ,

a. **Teaching us that**: The ancient Greek word for **teaching** has in mind what a parent does for a child. It speaks of the entire training process: teaching, encouragement, correction, and discipline. Grace is a teacher in this sense.

i. "'It teaches us' declares that grace also operates in the lives of the saved. Grounded in God's nature, grace makes ethical demands of Christians consistent with his nature. 'Teaches' pictures grace, practically personified, as instructing the believer in the things 'in accord with sound doctrine.'" (Hiebert)

ii. "He means that God's grace, should instruct us to order our lives aright. Some are quick to turn the preaching of God's mercy into an excuse for licentiousness, while carelessness keeps others from thinking about the renewal of their life. But the revelation of God's grace necessarily brings with it exhortations to a godly life." (Calvin)

iii. "Thus you see that grace has its own disciples. Are you a disciple of the grace of God? Did you ever come and submit yourself to it?" (Spurgeon)

b. **Denying ungodliness and worldly lusts**: Grace puts **ungodliness** and **worldly lusts** in our past. Now grace teaches us to renounce those things, not only to avoid them.

i. **Denying**: "This indicates the renunciation of the Devil, of the vanity of this world, and of all the sinful lusts of the flesh." (White)

ii. One may say that in a world where we are tempted to say "Yes" to every desire and feelings, that the reality of our faith can be demonstrated by what we say *no* to, by what we are willing to deny.

iii. "The most difficult part of the training of young men is not to put the right thing into them, but to get the wrong thing out of them." (Spurgeon)

c. **We should live soberly, righteously, and godly in the present age**:
Grace teaches us how to live **in the present age**. We must **live soberly**
(self-controlled) in regard to ourselves. We must live **righteously** in regard
to the people around us. And we must live **godly** ("to take God seriously")
in regard to our God.

i. "We are taught by that gentle school-mistress, the Grace of God, to
live – soberly, as regards our personal life; righteously, in relation to
others; godly, in our attitude towards God." (Meyer)

ii. Taken together, we see that the fear of the legalist – that preaching
grace produces Christians indifferent to obedience – is unfounded.
Grace teaches us obedience. "Wherever the grace of God comes
effectually, it makes the loose liver deny the desires of the flesh; it causes
the man who lusted after gold to conquer his greediness; it brings the
proud man away from his ambitions; it trains the idler to diligence,
and it sobers the wanton mind which cared only for the frivolities of
life. Not only do we leave these lusts, but we deny them." (Spurgeon)

iii. The phrase **godly in the present age** is also a subtle proof against
the idea of purgatory or some place of cleansing in the life to come.
"Not supposing that any thing will be purified in the world to come
that is not cleansed in this." (Clarke)

d. **Looking for the blessed hope**: Grace teaches us to expect and prepare
for our **blessed hope**. That **hope** is not heaven or glory, but Jesus Himself,
face to face, closer than ever.

i. **Looking for** indicates that Christians should live in active expectation
of the return of Jesus. It should be precious for Christians to consider:

- He came the first time to save the soul of man; He will come a
second time to resurrect the body.

- He came the first time to save the individual; He will come a
second time to save society.

- He came the first time to a crucifixion; He will come a second
time to a coronation.

- He came the first time to a tree; He will come a second time to a
throne.

- He came the first time in humility; He will come a second time
in glory.

- He came the first time and was judged by men; He will come a
second time to judge all men.

- He came the first time and stood before Pilate; He will come a second time and Pilate will stand before Him.

ii. **Our great God**: "This is the only place in the N.T. in which *megas* is applied to the true God, although it is a constant predicate of heathen gods and goddesses, *e.g.*, Acts 19:28." (White)

iii. "The discipline of grace, according to the apostle, has three results – denying, living, looking. You see the three words before you." (Spurgeon)

3. (14) The heart of the God of grace.

Who gave Himself for us, that He might redeem us from every lawless deed and purify for Himself *His* own special people, zealous for good works.

a. **Who gave Himself for us**: Every word of this description of Jesus' work is important. Jesus **gave**, which means it was voluntary. He gave **Himself**, which means Jesus gave all He could give. And He gave Himself **for us**, which means Jesus was given as a substitute for sinful man.

b. **That He might redeem us**: Redemption means "to be bought out of slavery by the paying of a ransom." We are bought out of our slavery to sin, and purchased *for* His service.

i. **From every lawless deed**: "And we are, therefore, taught that the death of Jesus was intended, not for our forgiveness and justification merely, but for our sanctification, and our deliverance from the power of all our besetting sins." (Meyer)

ii. **His own special people**: "The word we have translated *special* (*periousios*) is interesting. It means *reserved for*; and it was specially used for that part of the spoils of a battle or a campaign which the king who had conquered set apart especially for himself." (Barclay)

c. **Zealous for good works**: We are redeemed purchased to live with zeal. This is zeal with knowledge, and zeal for righteousness in our own life before zeal for righteousness in the lives of others.

i. "As you know, Titus was a teacher of teachers. He had to set in order the things that were wanting, and to show other preachers how they were to preach... You see how much of the Epistle is taken up with the affairs of ordinary life, matters of holy practice; so let our preaching be, and let Christian people learn to receive joyfully such instruction." (Spurgeon)

4. (15) The messengers of grace.

Speak these things, exhort, and rebuke with all authority. Let no one despise you.

a. **Speak these things**: Titus, and every one of God's messengers of grace are directed to speak, **exhort, and rebuke** - and to do it **with all authority**. God's messengers are to remember that they are messengers from a King, holding the word that brings life and turns back hell.

b. **Let no one despise you**: If Titus spoke **with all authority**, he had to back it up with his life. Titus had to live so that no one would **despise** him or his message.

i. "Since this letter would be read in the churches, the remark was apparently intended as much for the Cretans as for Titus himself." (Hiebert)

Titus 3 - Remember This

A. Remember good works.

1. (1-2) Remember to live obedient and kind lives.

Remind them to be subject to rulers and authorities, to obey, to be ready for every good work, to speak evil of no one, to be peaceable, gentle, showing all humility to all men.

> a. **Remind them**: In the grammar of the ancient Greek text, **remind** is in the present tense: "Go on reminding." Titus was to constantly remind the Christians under his care to show proper respect and humility towards all people, particularly those in a position of authority.

> > i. Knowing the sometimes difficult character of the people of Crete (as mentioned before in Titus 1:12), this command to **be subject to rulers and authorities** had special meaning.

> > ii. "It is perhaps significant of the difference between Crete and the province of Asia, as regards respect for law, that in 1 Timothy 2:1-3, reasons are given why we should pray for rulers, while here the more elementary duty of obedience is enjoined." (White)

> b. **Ready for every good work**: If we simply focus on being **subject to rulers and authorities**, it is easy to make the Christian life *passive*. Titus should not allow this, and also **remind them** to be **ready for every good work**.

> c. **Speak evil of no one... peaceable... gentle, showing all humility to all men**: This is a distinctively Christian kindness, coming not from simple good manners but from knowing who we are and who others are in the heart of Jesus.

2. (3) Remember what you used to be.

For we ourselves were also once foolish, disobedient, deceived, serving various lusts and pleasures, living in malice and envy, hateful and hating one another.

> a. **For we ourselves were also once**: This shows *why* Titus should *remind them* of the things mentioned in Titus 3:1-2. Remembering where we once were shows us that the fallen nature is not so far from us, and we need constant reminding to stay where we should be in the Lord.

> > i. **For we ourselves**: "You need not suppose that it is hopeless to imagine that these wild Cretan folk can be reclaimed. We ourselves are a living proof of the power of God's grace." (White)

> b. **Were also once foolish, disobedient, deceived**: Remembering this work of God builds four things in us.

> - First, *gratitude* for how God changed us.

> - Second, *humility* as we see that it was His work that changed us.

> - Third, *kindness* to others in the same place.

> - Finally, *faith* that God can change those who are still in that place.

3. (4-8) Remember the great salvation of God.

But when the kindness and the love of God our Savior toward man appeared, not by works of righteousness which we have done, but according to His mercy He saved us, through the washing of regeneration and renewing of the Holy Spirit, whom He poured out on us abundantly through Jesus Christ our Savior, that having been justified by His grace we should become heirs according to the hope of eternal life. This is a faithful saying, and these things I want you to affirm constantly, that those who have believed in God should be careful to maintain good works. These things are good and profitable to men.

> a. **But when the kindness and the love of God our Savior toward man appeared**: When we were in the place described by Titus 3:3, we didn't rescue ourselves. We were rescued by **the kindness and the love of God**. He reached out to us long before we reached out to Him.

> b. **Not by works of righteousness which we have done**: Our salvation isn't based on any **works of righteousness which we have done**. In and of itself, response to an altar call does not save. Saying the sinner's prayer does not save. Baptism does not save. Church attendance does not save. Giving does not save. Reading the Bible does not save. Each of these may be wonderful **works of righteousness**, but they do not save us. Instead, **according to His mercy He saved us.**

c. **He saved us**: This is the essence and distinctive of the gospel. We can notice the emphasis: **of God... not by works... His mercy... He saved us... of the Holy Spirit... He poured... through Jesus... by His grace... heirs**. God is always the initiator, and we receive from Him before we give anything back.

d. **Through the washing of regeneration**: These words are commonly taken as a reference to baptism, and this passage is sometimes quoted in support of the idea of *baptismal regeneration*. Yet we cannot say that Paul specifically mentions baptism here, and the only other use of the ancient Greek word translated **washing** here is connected with the *spiritual* cleansing of the believer by the Word of God through faith (Ephesians 5:26).

i. "In the LXX the word, which occurs three times only, on each occasion seems to represent not the receptacle but the washing itself. This is also the sense in the only other New Testament occurrence, Ephesians 5:26, 'the washing of water by the word.'" (Guthrie)

ii. "Most commentators take the washing as a reference to water baptism. But if water baptism is the means that produces the spiritual rebirth, we then have the questionable teaching of a material agency as the indispensable means for producing a spiritual result (but cf. Matthew 15:1-20; Romans 2:25-29; Galatians 5:6). We accept the washing as a divine inner act, although the experience is viewed as openly confessed before men in baptism." (Hiebert)

e. **Those who have believed in God should be careful to maintain good works**: This reminds us what we are saved *for* - **to maintain good works**. Faith alone saves, but the faith that saves is not alone. We must never put the cart of works before the horse of grace!

i. "The theology of Christianity is based on grace; the ethics of Christianity are based on gratitude." (Briscoe)

4. (9-11) Remember to keep on course.

But avoid foolish disputes, genealogies, contentions, and strivings about the law; for they are unprofitable and useless. Reject a divisive man after the first and second admonition, knowing that such a person is warped and sinning, being self-condemned.

a. **Avoid foolish disputes**: These are some of the things which ought not to be taught warned against in Titus 1:11. These **foolish disputes** are simply **unprofitable and useless**. Instead, Titus should focus on the simple word of God.

i. **Avoid**: "The word *peristemi* literally meaning to turn oneself about so as to face the other way (cf. 2 Timothy 2:16 where it is used in a similar manner)." (Guthrie)

ii. "The Jewish Rabbis spent their time building up imaginary genealogies for the characters of the Old Testament.... It is much easier to discuss theological questions than to be kind and considerate and helpful at home, or efficient and diligent and honest at work." (Barclay)

b. **Reject a divisive man**: Titus must take measures against those who insist on going their own way. Their self-will makes them **self-condemned**.

i. "Labour to convince him of his error; but if he will not receive instruction, if he has shut his heart against conviction, then – *burn him alive?* No, even if demonstrably a heretic in any one sense of that word, and a disturber of the peace of the church, God gives no man any other authority over him but to *shun him*. Do him no harm in body, soul, character, or substance; hold no communion with him; but leave him to God." (Clarke)

B. Concluding thoughts.

1. (12-13) Remember people.

When I send Artemas to you, or Tychicus, be diligent to come to me at Nicopolis, for I have decided to spend the winter there. Send Zenas the lawyer and Apollos on their journey with haste, that they may lack nothing.

a. **Artemas... Tychicus... Zenas... Apollos**: These personal words of Paul - common at the end of his letters - may seem insignificant, but are really very important. They communicate that Paul was a real man in a real world with real friends that he had regular contact with and care for.

i. "It is natural to suppose Artemas or Tychicus would take the place of Titus as apostolic legate in Crete. This temporary exercise of apostolic superintendence marks a stage in the development of monarchial local episcopacy in the later sense." (White)

ii. "The epistle closes with reference to Tychicus, Apollos, Artemas, and Zenas. The very mention of these names indicates the growth of the Christian movement." (Morgan)

b. **That they may lack nothing**: "The final word concerning occupation shows clearly the duty of members of the Christian Church to contribute to the support of those devoted to the work of the ministry." (Morgan)

2. (14-15) Remember to do good deeds.

And let our *people* also learn to maintain good works, to *meet* urgent needs, that they may not be unfruitful. All who *are* with me greet you. Greet those who love us in the faith. Grace *be* with you all. Amen.

a. **That they may not be unfruitful**: This is a recurring theme through Paul's letter to Titus. Paul was concerned that Christians might be barren and unfruitful, yet still have a "wonderfully" confident assurance of their standing in the Lord. Instead of being **unfruitful**, God's people must **learn to maintain good works** and **to meet urgent needs**.

b. **Grace be with you all**: "The closing benediction harmonizes with the opening salutation. It is a benediction of grace, the only difference being that whereas at the beginning it was addressed to Titus, at the close all those to whom he ministered were included." (Morgan)

Philemon - Paul's Plea to a Friend, on Behalf of a Slave

"This is a notable Epistle, and full of worth; each word having its weight, each syllable its substance. From an abject subject, the receiving of a runaway servant, St. Paul soars like a heavenly eagle, and flies a high pitch of heavenly discourse." (John Trapp)

A. Greeting and introduction.

1. (1) The writer and the recipient.

Paul, a prisoner of Christ Jesus, and Timothy *our* brother, To Philemon our beloved *friend* and fellow laborer,

a. **Paul, a prisoner**: This brief letter was written by Paul during his Roman imprisonment described in Acts 28:30-31. There are some that believe he wrote it from time of imprisonment in Ephesus, but this is an unlikely possibility.

b. **A prisoner of Christ Jesus**: As always, Paul did not consider himself a prisoner of Rome, of circumstances, or of the religious leaders who started his legal troubles (Acts 23-24). Paul was **a prisoner of Jesus Christ**.

i. "They were not shackles which self had riveted, but a chain with which Christ had invested him; thus they were a badge of office." (Lightfoot, cited by Oesterley)

c. **To Philemon our beloved friend**: Paul wrote to **Philemon**, a Christian brother living in Colosse. This is the only place in the New Testament where **Philemon** is mentioned by name, but we do know that he was a **beloved friend** to Paul.

i. Paul's friendship with Philemon is shown by something significantly *missing* in his greeting. Of the 13 letters Paul wrote to churches or individuals, in 9 of them he called himself an *apostle* in the opening verse. In this letter (along with Philippians and 1 and 2 Thessalonians), Paul appealed to his reader more as a friend and less an apostle.

2. (2-3) Greetings to the household of Philemon.

To the beloved Apphia, Archippus our fellow soldier, and to the church in your house: Grace to you and peace from God our Father and the Lord Jesus Christ.

a. **To the beloved Apphia: Apphia** was probably the wife of Philemon, and **Archippus** was probably his son. This address to family members is unique among the letters of Paul, but it makes sense considering the content of the letter to Philemon. In this letter Paul will appeal to Philemon regarding a runaway slave who has met Jesus and found refuge with Paul. In the customs of that day, Philemon's wife **Apphia** was the supervisor of the slaves in the household, so the letter concerned her also.

i. Regarding the escaped slave, "She is as much a party to the decision as her husband, because according to the custom of the time, she had day-to-day responsibility for the slaves." (Rupprecht)

b. **To the church in your house**: This means that the church – or a portion of the church – in Colosse met in the **house** of Philemon. The earliest Christians had no property of their own for church buildings. The Jews had their synagogues, but Christians met in the homes of their members. The Christians of a city would be gathered into different "house churches" with a city "bishop" overseeing the different house churches. House churches are also mentioned in Romans 16:5 and Colossians 4:15.

i. "Up to the third century we have no certain evidence of the existence of church buildings for the purpose of worship; all references point to private houses for this. In Rome several of the oldest churches appear to have been built on the sites of houses used for Christian worship." (Oesterley)

ii. Spurgeon points out that apparently, Philemon had a church that met in his house. This suggests to believers that *their* homes should also be a church, and that each home can have the characteristics of a healthy church:

- Consisting of converted, saved people.
- Worshipping together.
- Together having a bond of unity.
- Supplied with oversight.
- Teaching always present.

- With a heart to minister to those on the outside.

c. **Grace to you and peace**: Paul gave his customary greeting of **grace** and **peace**, found in each one of his letters. However, this greeting was not directed towards an entire congregation, but to Philemon as an individual. This makes the letter unique among Paul's writings.

> i. The other Pastoral Epistles (1 and 2 Timothy and Titus) are also written first to individuals, but the character of their content suggests that they were intended to be shared with the entire congregation. Philemon really is a personal note written by Paul to one man.
>
> ii. "It is only one sample of numberless letters which must have been written to his many friends and disciples by one of St Paul's eager temperament and warm affections, in the course of a long and chequered life." (Lightfoot)

3. (4-7) Paul's thanks God for Philemon.

I thank my God, making mention of you always in my prayers, hearing of your love and faith which you have toward the Lord Jesus and toward all the saints, that the sharing of your faith may become effective by the acknowledgment of every good thing which is in you in Christ Jesus. For we have great joy and consolation in your love, because the hearts of the saints have been refreshed by you, brother.

a. **I thank my God, making mention of you always in my prayers**: Paul prayed often for Philemon, and he prayed with thanksgiving to God. Philemon had been such a blessing to Paul that prayed often and gratefully for him.

> i. In Paul's letters, four times he says he *makes mention* for people: To the Romans (Romans 1:9), to the Ephesians (Ephesians 1:16), to the Thessalonians (1 Thessalonians 1:2), and here at Philemon 4.
>
> ii. **Making mention** means that Paul did not always pray long, intricate prayers for Philemon, but he did often make **mention** of Philemon in his prayers.

b. **Hearing of your love and faith**: Paul thanked God for Philemon because of his **love and faith** – first towards Jesus and then towards **all the saints**. The word "**saints**" in the New Testament describes *every* true Christian, not just *a few exceptional* Christians.

c. **That the sharing of your faith**: Paul prayed *for* Philemon, desiring that **the sharing** of his **faith** would **become effective** as Philemon understood the work God did in him (**every good thing which is in you**).

i. This is the foundation for all effective evangelism: the overflow of a life touched and changed by God. God had done **every good thing** in the life of Philemon. Now, it was a matter of it being *acknowledged* by both Philemon and those he shared the faith with. When these good things were understood, others would come to Jesus. The reason why some **sharing of the faith** in not **effective** is because we don't *know* or can't *communicate* **every good thing** God has done for us.

ii. **The sharing of your faith**: It is possible that Paul means the **sharing** of material things, prompted by **faith**. The ancient Greek word for **sharing** is *koinonia*, and sometimes Paul used *koinonia*, which means "fellowship, sharing," to describe giving (2 Corinthians 8:4; 9:13; Romans 15:6).

iii. "The apostle speaks here of the works of charity in which Philemon abounded toward poor Christians." (Clarke)

d. **Because the hearts of the saints have been refreshed by you, brother**: Paul remembered how wonderfully Philemon had met the needs of other Christians. He effectively **refreshed** the **hearts** of others.

B. Paul's plea on behalf of Onesimus.

1. (8-11) Paul speaks to Philemon regarding Onesimus

Therefore, though I might be very bold in Christ to command you what is fitting, *yet* **for love's sake I rather appeal** *to you*—**being such a one as Paul, the aged, and now also a prisoner of Jesus Christ—I appeal to you for my son Onesimus, whom I have begotten** *while* **in my chains, who once was unprofitable to you, but now is profitable to you and to me.**

a. **Therefore, though I might be very bold in Christ to command you what is fitting, yet for love's sake I rather appeal**: It is clear that Paul will ask a favor of Philemon. Before he asked, he appealed **for love's sake** instead of making a **command**. Of course, under the surface Paul made it clear that he had the *right* to **command you what is fitting** – yet he appealed in **love**.

i. A loving appeal is often better than an authoritative command. Paul wasn't hesitant to command when the situation demanded it (1 Corinthians 5:4-5), but in wisdom he knew when to use the loving appeal.

b. **Being such a one as Paul, the aged, and now also a prisoner of Jesus Christ**: It was clear Paul would ask a favor of Philemon. Before he asked, he appealed to Philemon's sympathies by the way he described himself (**Paul, the aged**) and his circumstances (**a prisoner**).

i. Since Paul will make his appeal based on love, he does what he can to stir up the loving sympathy of Philemon. "Philemon, before I tell you what I need from you, remember that I'm an old man, and a prisoner at that."

ii. Some translations have *ambassador* instead of **aged**. There is a difference of one letter between the two ancient Greek words.

c. **I appeal to you for my son Onesimus**: Onesimus was an escaped slave who escaped from his master Philemon. It seems that when **Onesimus** escaped, he fled to Rome and – intentionally or not – met with Paul. Paul, though under house arrest by the Romans, led **Onesimus** to faith in Jesus Christ (**whom I have begotten while in my chains**).

i. It was logical that **Onesimus** escaped to Rome, the biggest city of the Roman Empire. Lightfoot says, "Rome was the natural cesspool for these offscourings of humanity." But at his providential meeting of Paul in Rome, **Onesimus** met the man who had led his master Philemon to Jesus (Philemon 19).

ii. When Paul made this appeal on behalf of **Onesimus**, he followed deep traditions in Roman culture. There was an ancient Greek law (inherited by the Romans) allowing any escaped slave sanctuary at an altar. The altar could even be the hearth of a private family home; then the head of the family was obligated to give the slave protection while he tried to persuade him to return to his master. If the slave refused, the head of the family would put the slave up for auction and give the price for the slave to the former master. Paul gave **Onesimus** protection, and now was working the issue out with Philemon.

d. **My son Onesimus**: Paul often spoke of his converts as his "children." Timothy (1 Corinthians 4:17), Titus (Titus 1:4), the Corinthian Christians (1 Corinthians 4:14) and the Galatian Christians (Galatians 4:19) were each called Paul's "children."

e. **Who once was unprofitable to you, but now is profitable to you and to me**: In some way, Onesimus became **profitable** to Paul. Perhaps he served as an assistant to Paul during his house arrest. So, Philemon's runaway slave Onesimus was now **unprofitable** to Philemon since he had escaped. But he had become **profitable** to Paul – and by extension, also to Philemon (**profitable to you and me**). Since Philemon loved Paul, if Onesimus helped Paul he was helping Philemon also.

i. When Paul spoke of Onesimus being **unprofitable** and **profitable**, he made a play on a word. The name **Onesimus** means *profitable*. Now that he was a Christian, Onesimus could live up to his name

ii. "It is significant to note that Paul claims that in Christ the useless person has been made useful." (Barclay)

iii. By making this clear to Philemon, Paul gently hinted that he would like to retain the services of this escaped slave – though he would not *command* Philemon to do this.

2. (12-14) Paul sends Onesimus back with the hope that Philemon will allow him to return again to Paul.

I am sending him back. You therefore receive him, that is, my own heart, whom I wished to keep with me, that on your behalf he might minister to me in my chains for the gospel. But without your consent I wanted to do nothing, that your good deed might not be by compulsion, as it were, but voluntary.

a. **I am sending him back. You therefore receive him, that is, my own heart**: Onesimus had done something wrong in that he escaped from his master. It was time to set that right, so Paul was willing to send **him back**. Yet Paul obviously wanted Philemon to deal gently with Onesimus. Under Roman law the slave owner had complete and total control over his slave. It wasn't unusual for slaves to be crucified for lesser offenses than escaping.

i. One ancient writer described how a slave carried a tray of crystal goblets, and he dropped and broke one. The master instantly demanded the slave be thrown into a fishpond full of lampreys that tore the slave to pieces. "Roman law... practically imposed no limits to the power of the master over his slave. The alternative of life or death rested solely with Philemon, and slaves were constantly crucified for far lighter offenses than this." (Lightfoot)

ii. Considering the huge number of slaves in the Roman Empire, they thought the harsh punishment against escaped or rebellious slaves was necessary. In an Empire with as many as 60 million slaves, there were constant fears of a slave revolt. Therefore, laws against runaways were strict. When captured, a runaway slave might be crucified, or branded with a red-hot iron on the forehead with the letter "F" for *fugitive*.

iii. Considering this, we understand Paul's phrase **that is, my own heart**. "Philemon, I know this man has done you wrong and deserves to be punished. But consider him as **my own heart** and be merciful to him."

b. **Whom I wished to keep with me, that on your behalf he might minister to me in my chains for the gospel**: Clearly, Paul wanted Onesimus to stay, because he had become a big help. Paul sweetened his appeal in three ways.

i. First, if Onesimus stayed he could serve Paul **on your behalf**. "Philemon, if you leave Onesimus with me, it's like *you* serving me, because Onesimus is your rightful servant."

ii. Secondly, if Onesimus stayed he helped a man in **chains**. "Philemon, I know Onesimus might be of some use to you. Yet I am in **chains** and need all the help I can get."

iii. Thirdly, if Onesimus stayed he helped man in **chains for the gospel**. "Philemon, please don't forget why I am here in **chains**. Remember that it is for the sake of the **gospel**."

c. **But without your consent I wanted to do nothing**: Paul made his appeal and made it strong and skillfully. At the same time, he really did leave the decision to Philemon. He would appeal in love, but he would not trample over the rights of Philemon.

d. **That your good deed might not be by compulsion, as it were, but voluntary**: This explained why Paul would not force a decision on Philemon. If Paul *demanded* it, then Philemon's **good deed** would come by **compulsion**, and not be **voluntary**. This would make the whole affair unpleasant and rob Philemon of any reward he otherwise might have had.

i. Essentially, Paul gave Philemon the freedom to do what was right in love before the Lord, and he gave the freedom to do it on his own choice and not out of Paul's compulsion.

3. (15-16) Paul explains the providential hand of God at work in Onesimus' escape.

For perhaps he departed for a while for this *purpose*, that you might receive him forever, no longer as a slave but more than a slave—a beloved brother, especially to me but how much more to you, both in the flesh and in the Lord.

a. **Departed for a while**: It was true that Philemon **departed**, but Paul would send him back. Somehow **departed for a while** doesn't sound nearly as bad as *escaped slave*.

i. In writing **departed for a while**, Paul spoke softly of a slave's escape. Clarke said of this phrase, "This is another most delicate stroke."

b. **For perhaps he departed for a while for this purpose**: In some ways the escape of Onesimus was nothing but trouble. It deprived Philemon of a worker and an asset. It made Onesimus a criminal, possibly subject to the death penalty. Yet in it all, Paul could see a **purpose** of God and he wanted Philemon to see the **purpose** also.

i. The phrase, "**for perhaps**" is important. It showed that Paul did not come to Philemon in this manner: "Philemon, God has shown me His hidden hand at work, and you must accept what I see also." Instead, **for perhaps** means Paul's heart is like this: "Philemon, it seems to me that God is working in unusual ways here. Let me tell you what I see, and **perhaps** it will make sense to you."

c. **That you may receive him forever**: This was one aspect of the **purpose** Paul saw God working in the escape of Onesimus. Philemon the master lost a slave; but Philemon the Christian gained a brother, and he gained that brother **forever**.

i. "Here the apostle makes the best of an ill-matter. Converts are to be gently handled, and their former evil practices not to be aggravated." (Trapp)

d. **That you might receive him forever, no longer as a slave but more than a slave; a beloved brother**: Paul "re-introduced" Onesimus to Philemon; not as a slave, but as a brother. In this relationship as brothers and not slaves, Paul effectively abolished the sting of the "master-slave" relationship and laid the foundation for the eventual legal abolition of slavery. If a man is a stranger, I might make him my slave. But how can my brother be my slave?

i. This breaking of the distinction between master and slave was an absolutely revolutionary development. It did far more to change society than the passing of a law prohibiting slavery.

ii. "What the letter to Philemon does is to bring the institution into an atmosphere where it could only wilt and die. Where master and slave were united in affection as brothers in Christ, formal emancipation would be but a matter of expediency, the legal confirmation of their new relationship." (Bruce)

iii. The transformation of the *individual* is the key to the transformation of society and the moral environment. "But mark this word, - the true reforming of the drunkard lies in giving him a new heart; the true reclaiming of the harlot is to be found in a renewed nature.... I see certain of my brethren fiddling away at the branches of the tree of vice with their wooden saws, but, as for the gospel, it lays the axe at the roots of the whole forest of evil, and if it be fairly received into the heart it fells all the bad trees at once, and instead of them there spring up the fir tree, the pine tree, and the box tree together, to beautify the house of our Master's glory." (Spurgeon)

4. (17-19) Paul's personal promise of restitution towards Philemon.

If then you count me as a partner, receive him as *you would* me. But if he has wronged you or owes anything, put that on my account. I, Paul, am writing with my own hand. I will repay—not to mention to you that you owe me even your own self besides.

a. **If then you count me as a partner, receive him as you would me**: Again, Paul stood beside Onesimus, requesting mercy. "If I am your partner in the gospel, then treat Onesimus like you would treat me."

i. Paul's appeal is powerful because he stood beside a guilty man and said to the owner of the slave, "I know this man is a criminal and deserves punishment. Yet this slave is my friend, so if you punish him punish me also. I stand beside him to take his punishment." This is what Jesus does for us before our master, God the Father.

b. **But if he has wronged you or owes anything, put that on my account**: Apparently when Onesimus escaped he also stole from Philemon. This in itself was a capital crime. Paul asked that the value of what had been stolen be "charged" to Paul's **account**. "Put it on my tab, Philemon."

c. **I, Paul, am writing with my own hand. I will repay**: Paul was so serious about that he gave Philemon a personal IOU, written by his own hand. When Paul said to Philemon, "charge the wrong of Onesimus to my account," he essentially did for Onesimus what Jesus did for us in taking our sins to *His* account.

i. "Here we see how Paul lays himself out for poor Onesimus, and with all his means pleads his cause with his master, and so sets himself as if he were Onesimus, and had himself done wrong to Philemon. Even as Christ did for us with God the Father, thus also does Paul for Onesimus with Philemon. We are all his Onesimi, to my thinking." (Luther)

d. **Not to mention to you that you owe me even your own self besides**: While "accounts" were being studied, Paul mentioned one more thing. "Philemon, remember that I have a lot of credit on your account, because you **owe me even your own self besides**." Paul could afford to pay Onesimus' expenses because there was a sense in which Philemon owed Paul his salvation!

5. (20-22) Paul's confidence in Philemon's response.

Yes, brother, let me have joy from you in the Lord; refresh my heart in the Lord. Having confidence in your obedience, I write to you, knowing that you will do even more than I say. But, meanwhile, also prepare a guest room for me, for I trust that through your prayers I shall be granted to you.

a. **Let me have joy from you in the Lord**: **Joy** is more literally *profit*. It translates the ancient Greek word *oninemi*, the root word for the name "Onesimus." Paul used another play on words and the name Onesimus to communicate a not so subtle request: "Let me have Onesimus back from you in the Lord."

b. **Refresh my heart in the Lord**: Earlier in the letter, Paul said that Philemon was a man who refreshed the heart of the saints (Philemon 7). Now, he specifically told Philemon how he could refresh Paul's heart: by allowing Onesimus to stay with Paul.

c. **Knowing that you will do even more than I say**: Paul's letter, full of appeal, was also full of hope. Philemon was not a bad or a harsh man. Paul had every reason to expect that he would fulfill his Christian duty and **do even more than** Paul asked.

d. **But, meanwhile, also prepare a guest room for me**: This showed the close relationship between Paul and Philemon. Paul knew that hospitality always waited for him at Philemon's home.

e. **I trust that through your prayers I shall be granted to you**: Paul wanted Philemon to pray, and he didn't think the prayers were a mere formality. Paul believed that it would be **through** the **prayers** of Philemon that they would once again be together.

C. Conclusion.

1. (23-24) Paul sends greetings to Philemon from common friends in Rome.

Epaphras, my fellow prisoner in Christ Jesus, greets you, *as do* **Mark, Aristarchus, Demas, Luke, my fellow laborers.**

a. **Ephaphras... Mark... Aristachus... my fellow laborers**: Each of these names is also mentioned in the conclusion of the letter to the Colossians (Colossians 4:10-17). This confirms that the two letters went to the same place. Philemon lived in Colosse.

i. **Fellow prisoner**: "Literally 'a prisoner of war,' used metaphorically." (Oesterley)

b. **Demas**: "*Demas* is supposed to be the same who continued in his attachment to Paul till his last imprisonment at Rome: after which he left him for what is supposed to have been the *love of the world*, 2 Timothy 4:10." (Clarke)

2. (25) Conclusion to the letter.

The grace of our Lord Jesus Christ *be* **with your spirit. Amen.**

a. **The grace of the Lord Jesus Christ be with your spirit**: We see some enduring principles from Paul's letter to Philemon.

i. *Paul never called for an overthrow of the system of slavery, yet the principles in the letter to Philemon destroy slavery.* The greatest social changes come when people are changed, one heart at a time. In our society, racism and our low regard for the unborn cannot be eliminated by laws; a change of heart must occur.

ii. *Onesimus was obligated to return to his master.* When we do something wrong, we must do our best to set it right. Being made a *new creation* in Christ (2 Corinthians 5:17) does not end our responsibility to make restitution; it increases our obligation, even when restitution is difficult.

iii. *Onesimus was morally responsible for his wrongs.* The letter to Philemon demonstrates that we are *not* primarily directed by economics, despite the ideas of Marxists and modern liberals. Whether rich or poor, we are to be directed by the Spirit of God, not our economic status.

iv. "No part of the New Testament more clearly demonstrates integrated Christian thinking and living. It offers a blend, utterly characteristic of Paul, of love, wisdom, humour, gentleness, tact, and above all Christian and human maturity." (Wright)

b. **Amen**: The conclusion of the letter can lead us to ask, "Why is the letter to Philemon in our Bibles?" In A.D. 110, the bishop of Ephesus was named Onesimus, and it could have been this same man. If Onesimus was in his late teens or early twenties when Paul wrote this letter, he would then be about 70 years old in A.D. 110 and that was not an unreasonable age for a bishop in those days.

i. "Ignatius, in his Epistle to the Ephesians, maketh mention of Onesimus, as pastor of Ephesus, next after Timothy. The Roman Martyrologue saith, that he was stoned to death at Rome, under Trajan the emperor." (Trapp)

ii. There is also some historical evidence that the letters of Paul were first gathered as a group in the city of Ephesus. Perhaps Onesimus first compiled the letters and wanted to make sure *his* letter – his charter of freedom – was included.

Bibliography - 1-2 Timothy, Titus, and Philemon

Alford, Henry *The New Testament for English Readers, Volume II, Part I* (London: Rivingtons, 1866)

Barclay, William *The Letters to Timothy, Titus, and Philemon* (Philadelphia: The Westminster Press, 1976)

Bruce, F.F. *The Epistles to the Colossians, to Philemon, and to the Ephesians* (Grand Rapids, Michigan: Eerdmans, 1984)

Calvin, John "The Second Epistle of Paul the Apostle to the Corinthians and the Epistles to Timothy, Titus, and Philemon," *Calvin's New Testament Commentaries, Volume 10* [Translator: A.W. T.A. Smail] (Grand Rapids, Michigan: Eerdmans, 1972)

Clarke, Adam *The New Testament of Our Lord and Saviour Jesus Christ, Volume II* (New York: Eaton & Mains, 1832)

Draper, James T. Jr. *Titus: Patterns for Church Living* (Wheaton, Illinois: Tyndale House, 1971)

Earle, Ralph "1, 2 Timothy," *The Expositor's Bible Commentary, Volume 11* (Grand Rapids, Michigan: Regency/Zondervan, 1978)

Guthrie, Donald *The Pastoral Epistles* (Leicester, England: Inter-Varsity Press, 1988)

Hannegraff, Hank *Counterfeit Revival* (Dallas, Texas: Word Publishing, 1997)

Hiebert, D. Edmond *First Timothy* (Chicago, Illinois: Moody Press, 1957)

Hiebert, D. Edmond *Second Timothy* (Chicago, Illinois: Moody Press, 1958)

Hiebert, D. Edmond "Titus," *The Expositor's Bible Commentary, Volume 11* (Grand Rapids, Michigan: Regency/Zondervan, 1978)

Ironside, H.A. *Timothy, Titus, and Philemon* (Neptune, New Jersey: Loizeaux Brothers, 1981)

Lightfoot, J.B. *St. Paul's Epistles to the Colossians and to Philemon* (Lynn, Massachusetts: Hendrickson Publishers, 1982)

Meyer, F.B. *Our Daily Homily* (Westwood, New Jersey: Revell, 1966)

Morgan, G. Campbell *An Exposition of the Whole Bible* (Old Tappan, New Jersey: Revell, 1959)

Morgan, G. Campbell *Searchlights from the Word* (New York: Revell, 1926)

Oesterley W.E. "The Epistle to Philemon," *The Expositor's Greek New Testament, Volume IV* (London: Hodder and Stoughton, ?)

Poole, Matthew *A Commentary on the Holy Bible, Volume III: Matthew-Revelation* (London: Banner of Truth Trust, 1969, first published in 1685)

Robertson, Archibald Thomas, *Word Pictures in the New Testament, Volume IV: The Epistles of Paul* (Nashville, Tennessee: Broadman Press, 1931)

Rupprecht, Arthur A. "Philemon," *The Expositor's Bible Commentary, Volume 11* (Grand Rapids, Michigan: Regency/Zondervan, 1978)

Spurgeon, Charles Haddon *The New Park Street Pulpit, Volumes 1-6* and *The Metropolitan Tabernacle Pulpit, Volumes 7-63* (Pasadena, Texas: Pilgrim Publications, 1990)

Stott, John R.W. *Guard the Gospel – the Message of 2 Timothy* (Downer's Grove, Illinois: InterVarsity Press, 1973)

Trapp, John *A Commentary on the Old and New Testaments, Volume Five* (Eureka, California: Tanski Publications, 1997)

White, Newport J.D. "The First and Second Epistles to Timothy" and "The Epistle to Titus," *The Expositor's Greek New Testament, Volume IV* (London: Hodder and Stoughton, ?)

Wiersbe, Warren W. *The Bible Exposition Commentary, Volume 2* (Wheaton, Illinois: Victor Books, 1989)

Wright, N.T. *Colossians and Philemon* (Leicester, England: Inter-Varsity Press, 1986)

As the years pass I love the work of studying, learning, and teaching the Bible more than ever. I'm so grateful that God is faithful to meet me in His Word.

Thanks once again to Debbie Pollaccia for her proofreading help. After so many years of her help, one might think I would better understand the workings of commas and semi-colons. I'm quite grateful for her patience, corrections, and suggestions. Thanks also to Brian Procedo for the cover design and all the graphics work.

Most especially, thanks to my wife Inga-Lill. She is my loved and valued partner in life and in service to God and His people.

David Guzik

David Guzik's Bible commentary is regularly used and trusted by many thousands who want to know the Bible better. Pastors, teachers, class leaders, and everyday Christians find his commentary helpful for their own understanding and explanation of the Bible. David and his wife Inga-Lill live in Santa Barbara, California.

You can email David at
david@enduringword.com

For more resources by David Guzik,
go to www.enduringword.com

CPSIA information can be obtained
at www.ICGtesting.com
Printed in the USA
BVHW082023050222
628090BV00003B/212